*THE PACIFIC NOR*

*POETRY SERIES*

Linda Bierds / *General Editor*

THE PACIFIC NORTHWEST

POETRY SERIES

# THE CORPSE FLOWER

NEW AND SELECTED POEMS

*BRUCE BEASLEY*

UNIVERSITY OF WASHINGTON PRESS

*SEATTLE & LONDON*

*The Corpse Flower*, the sixth volume in the
Pacific Northwest Poetry Series, is published with
the generous support of Cynthia Lovelace Sears.

University of Washington Press
P.O. Box 50096, Seattle, WA 98145
www.washington.edu/uwpress

Library of Congress Cataloging-in-Publication Data
Beasley, Bruce, 1958–
The corpse flower : new and selected poems / Bruce Beasley.
p. cm. — (The Pacific Northwest poetry series)
ISBN 0-295-98638-7 (hardback : alk. paper)
ISBN 0-295-98639-5 (pbk. : alk. paper)
I. Title.   II. Series.
PS3552.EI748C67 2006
811'.54—dc22                           2006015768

*For Susanne and Jin*

"*Jesus said: He who has known the world has found a corpse; and he who has found a corpse, the world is not worthy of him.*"
—The Gospel of Thomas


"*Why do you seek the living among the dead? Why do you mourn the incorrupt amid corruption?*"
—Orthodox Easter liturgy

# CONTENTS

# INITIALS

from *Spirituals* (1988), *The Creation* (1994),
and *Summer Mystagogia* (1996)

*forerunner*—

# *Witness*

I

*That's where your father*
*had his accident,* my father
mumbled, pointing

through the cracked windshield
to the dropoff where he'd plunged that car
into spiky shrubs thirty feet below.

But I knew
anyway from my mother's
enraged voice on the phone,

then from the barred
psychiatric ward,
it was no accident.

That gesture—his finger tracing
vaguely all he couldn't talk about—
comes back to me now, through

Caravaggio, where Christ
guides the apostle's pointing finger
with sexual tenderness

into the smooth, apparently permanent
gash in his breast.
Through his one sentence, my father's

voice was rough with such regret—
for having tried, or having failed,
I couldn't tell—

3

I only knew his scarred
arm on the steering wheel
scared me, and his sweet

whiskey breath, and the broken guardrail
stabbing its twisted metal
over the skidmarks still there down the edge . . .

I thought: he must have tried to make it stop.
But I didn't want to know,
didn't want to watch

his headlights scoop out that canyon
or the darkness fill it back up,
or his lips, lit by a cigarette stub,

try to tell me what had gone wrong
and I didn't say a thing
as he twisted the radio dial

from gospel to Muzak to static,
coughed his dry, frightened cough
and watched me from the side of his eye.

The torn seat squeaking on its hinges
was the only sound as we rumbled
down the brick streets of Macon

where I watched his back
disappear through glass
doors throbbing with dancing bottles.

2

In Caravaggio's painting, the voyeur
apostles throng
so close around Jesus and Thomas,

gazing hard as the fingertip
slips into the pucker of wound.
They all want to know what it's like

inside the cut, risen body,
but they're scared of what
the touch might do; it's assuring to watch

the curious one
penetrate first. But Thomas
is tense, his forehead ridged,

his throat tight as he goes
deeper into the fresh
opening just under the skin—

he's mortified, like one
admitted where he can never belong.
Still, Caravaggio has torn

the shoulder seam
on his red robe, which means
he's as human as Christ,

available to damage too. My father
died a year after that ride, and now
I don't even know

where the road he showed me
is. At fourteen, I closed my eyes
and let his old Nova

carry me home,
the Ocmulgee River's
smell of mud-clogged kudzu and swampgrass

washing over my father's Jack Daniels.
He turns back to me now,
when I want him to, lifts

his shaking hand to the window,
and points again down the cliff,
and the flesh–

colored robe opens, and the finger
pierces just under the heart,
and the hand with its nailhole coaxes

the bewildered witness in.

# The Creation of Eve

We lay a long time in the brine of my blood,

Father,
this other
hacked from my flesh,

her side by my gashed side.
Strangers—

How fitfully we slept like that, her hair
sponging the long cut
just under my throat.

We didn't speak, falling asleep, waking each other in starts—

both feverish. Once I dreamed
You were calling and calling and I
couldn't answer,
something caught deep on my tongue.

It was days
before we could eat; I split
a lopsided fruit and squeezed
the juice from its hundred
scarlet seeds
into her mouth—

That's all she could take. So weak,
after being
crushed into life in Your hands . . .

I never asked
for another, didn't know
what to say to her, what to do—

the first three days we just
gazed, not talking,
over the east side of the hill
where you can see all four of the rivers slipping
away from the garden (where
do they go?)—I laid
my head in her lap and she
hummed, and the sun
poured itself into the slow-moving water.

We watched
three horned birds
I'd never named
spiral above us,
black-winged and beaked, red-eyed—

Her skin
and mine both stained, and our hair—
like the sky, a red we'd never seen,
and the birds
splayed their wings and tilted
above us in rings, circling
down to the bloody
mulch of fig leaves where we

kneeled . . .

My Father,
I never thought
either of us
would heal—

# Eve, Learning to Speak

A world already *deposed*
in the urge of his stressed
consonants, vowels
slack:
*mood* and *doom* and *mudsink, logbridge*
and *pear,*
the gouge of the creek, hunched
leaves—

For days I called him *I,*

called the root in his fist
*water,* called what fire does
*bathe*—

He'd close me
for hours in the rivercliff
cave, to make me
remember, then he'd teach me
a name for that: *alone.*

Alone,
I practiced the unnatural sounds,
touching my lips as he did,
feeling air
move through my throat, my chest,
letting it stay there.

Then sometimes the hush, the thrill
of seeing things he hadn't
claimed yet with his tongue:
once I woke, wet, hands muddy,

to something quick and burning
cutting through the trees.
And pieces of river
clinging to the spiderswings
between the crimped, rough applelimbs:

I would have kept that
as it was, tangible, alien,
let the memory swell,
unsayable—
and I stared at him
refusing words
when he came to rescue me
and teach me *rain* and *lightning*.

But some things
I kept as my own: the hurt
low in my body
he knew nothing of.
I came to like it. And my own
name for the land, not a sound,
nothing any body could reproduce . . .

He wanted everything
common, so we could
*exchange* it, as though it were breath,
as though I still lay
deep in the bone and muscle of his side.

Sometimes I'd see myself
as I thought he must:
cut off, inviolable—
and I'd sit with him
and watch the high, cold grasses
all blowing one way.

I'd give in and let my strange
voice come.
And I'd feel the world diminishing, name by name,
as we talked through the long hours, and my new
life
hardened into form.

# Childhood

In Macon, the paper mill
used to fill the night air with a stench
before rain:
acrid, decayed, like burnt garbage.

I couldn't understand why weather
required such a warning, a burning off.

On the back porch in summer, the air
felt tense, expectant—
a siren sounding closer & closer to home,

two flies caught, & furious, in the torn screen,

the sharp-tipped
leaves pointing over the stormclouds.

Then a clearing: smell of mud in cement-cracks,
& each star exactly in its place around the pecan tree,

all hesitant & dim, quivering, waiting their time.

# Indian Summer

*—for my mother*


I pick a leaf from my childhood,

magnolia, hard-skinned green,
in late October,
Indian summer. Unreasonable

for such a leaf
to flourish now, its waxy hull
smoothed by rain,

its hard stem
propping it upward.
So lavish, in the sun,

with the other leaves
already discolored and the sky,
too, blackening around the edges.

We floated those leaves
down a dammed
creek when I was a child,

just to watch them
bob in the mud-colored water,
off-balance, off-green in the foam.

My mother's painting of a magnolia
curled in a white bloom
hangs at the top of my stairs now

warped in its frame, the rough
crust of the oils on the canvas.
In the first

summer I remember she stood
looking out the picture window, dust
swarming all around her in the sun,

watching those enormous flowers: the faint
yellow along their edges,
their olive seams.

She must have noticed, too,
the dingy brown
belly of each leaf, underneath

the gloss: one
in the painting is turned awkwardly
outward just to show it,

just to admit the flaw,
the twisted stem
cracking from the weight of the gesture.

That summer she told me each speck
of dust was the soul of someone
who'd died, floating up to heaven.

I watched them
climb in long arcs by the window
one drab Sunday afternoon,

then settle on my sleeve
or the mirror
as if they were determined to stay.

On the day of my mother's funeral
twenty years later, magnolias
bordered the highway, their leaves

tattered, shellacked, as we drove
from Rose Hill to the hospital where
my niece lay flushed behind glass,

born that same balmy
January afternoon.
I'd flown from a Cleveland blizzard

into Macon's damp, feverish
air, my mother dead of pneumonia.
Outside the air-conditioned car

those leaves hung fat and green,
glutted, as they are today, with sun,
too lush for the season . . .

Sometimes what's taken comes back
outside its time
to brush us again, *now* and *then*

streaming back together like a forked
creek when it pools at a dam, as
at this one still moment in October.

# Summer

Between the lilac and pink dogwood, by the shrunken fig,
   a field of poison oak

spread, choked with scuppernong and the sharp
cracked shells of pecans.
I crouched there, in thunder, at sundown, searching

for rattlesnakes
or dead bodies, glass shards, hidden mouths of caves.
Whatever it took to disturb

the ordinary
sounds and smells of summer: the swamp-black creek
at Moose Park,

horseshoes and Creedence Clearwater Revival
under the basketball hoop in floodlight,
my father, drunk at midnight,

watering the Cherokee rose
outside my window
for hours, whistling a sad, unnameable tune

as I lay wide awake in the crackling
of mosquito lights, the transistor
pressed to my ear

buzzing all night its staticky claims of love.

# The Instrument and Proper Corps of the Soule

*Yet is not this masse of flesh and visible structure
the instrument and proper corps of the soule . . .*
—Sir Thomas Browne, *Religio Medici*

I

My mother brought me, from the butcher's,

a brain
lumped and seeping in its plastic bag

for my fifth-grade science project.
I held it against the lamp,

traced its cerebellum and medulla,
the lobes and hemispheres and fleshy folds

in which a cow's world resided:
grassy fields spiked with fences,

creeks wallowing in kudzu. On our kitchen table
the World Book lay open to a transparency

of the brain—a sheet you'd lay
over the drawing of a body

that filled in the skull
and marked each of the senses: arrows

to the seat of vision, of memory, of rage.

2

In 1634, Sir Thomas Browne
dissected the human

brain but found
no organ there

to contain the soul,
only layers of tissue, inscrutably folded,

nothing he could not see
as easily in the cranium of a beast.

3

Across the gray fat, the synaptic clefts—

the grooved, fissured
depths of his infolded brain—

a blood-clot grew through my father's
last years, the slow strokes

toward insanity after years of liquor. Is that what gave
him such rage he'd hunt my mother

through the house *Let go of me children*
*you're letting her get away* . . .

I hardly said a word to him for years
till he'd corner me and bellow

*Goddammit are you mute*
and I'd turn away and shake my head.

4

Someone I love
has wept for days, for no reason, the skewed
signals in her brain, suck

of dopamine from the cells
making her want nothing
but to die.

—What
is the soul, that it
should surrender so abjectly
to the currents

and electrical misfirings of the flesh?

5

I don't know what the brain
can explain to us

when it burns
with all its life inside,

oxygen and blood gorging it,
clamoring to make sense of its signals.

Transmitters leaping through synapses
in the stalk

and hidden recesses of that flesh
determine too much of what we are:

my mother, in DTs, screaming
at my body flying over her bed

two months before vodka killed her.
It's what we can't see

that masters us, the mysteries
of blood and gods and brains

no matter how
carefully we try to graph them,

specify their parts, or hold them
carved and singled out for us, heft in our fists.

# At Easter

Now your going appears to us

suddenly, the hedge broken out
in white flowers overnight,
a pink scab along the bottom of each bloom.

Now, on the brown, opaque
lake-waves,
we close our eyes in sunlight,
lie down together in the boat's slosh.

There's something we keep wanting to feel,
looking over the hibiscus
shedding its blooms,
the pollen set loose in the sun . . .

You can smell it on every bush,
this hankering to get born:
yellowjackets and wasps drone after it all day

and larvae skim the dirty lake.
Tadpoles float on their bloated heads
in the shallow deadwater.

There's not a sign of you, who rose
from this breeding world in spring, knowing
if you took your body with you
you could never be touched again.

# The Reliquary

*I wait gluttonously for God.*—Arthur Rimbaud

All over Italy, the saints'
bodies are scattered, grizzled
and crumbling in glass cases,
brittle, barely
durable, St. Jerome's
one finger pointing the way.

There's a black
nail from Calvary, a sallow
shard of a wrist bone, cross–
splinters, and under
stained glass, huddled
figurines: Christ
half–risen, a wooden
Joseph and Mary
kneeling in their crèche

simple as a child's
prayer–slur before sleep, or the sure
words of a catechism
we barely recall.

And the canvases,
so casually
crowded with angels
and saints who bear,
too soon, their martyrdom:
Sebastian, already burdened
by arrows, attends
the Virgin and Child,
and Mary submits to the stern
angel, already

admitting the strange
embryo into her womb.

Over an altar, Titian's
Virgin luffs
into heaven, her red
robes trailing through the dim
church, the painting
left like a vestige of her body
that has so long been
withdrawn, abruptly
assumed . . .

If the body's a temple
of the Holy Ghost, the saints'
skeletons scattered piece by piece
from Palermo to Ravenna
are fallen
shrines like Michelangelo's
smashed Pieta,
locked like a relic behind glass
in St. Peter's,

glued together and still.

When we left
Santa Maria Novella, thousands of pigeons
swarmed, pecking for bread;
the square was empty and the moon
rose close to the church, the heavens
glossed over, opening and closing
through the clouds, with an eerie

backlight like the thick
glass of a reliquary, enclosing
the rich and secret odor of decay.

# Novice

I

After his nervous breakdown in the war,
after just six months at Pearl Harbor
discharged from the Marines,
after cruising Atlanta in his convertible Studebaker,
my father is 21,
anxious, his fingers
beating the hood of the car.
It's May, the dogwoods dying,
the marble and red tile
of the college blurring behind him.
He's on the verge
of what he doesn't know,
what I know now:
twenty-seven years
it took him to waste
his life away from his body:
alcoholic, manic-depressive, five children
afraid of his fists,
afraid of him
slumped in his chair,
smelling of liquor and cigarettes,
rattling the ice in his glass,
scribbling gibberish on legal pads.
He mapped highways through the houses
of families who cursed him—
condemned their land,
drove them into court.
Now the semis
haul their shadows down his highway,
letting them fall
over his grave by the river bridge.

Once I couldn't
find that grave, so many
new headstones had grown up around it.
So I prayed beside
another, as if any of them would do
to call back that haunted
face, harsh, smoothed by whiskey.
On summer afternoons
my mother and I would crouch,
brush the mowed grass off his name,
and lay down roses
we'd cut from our yard.
"I think it's silly anyway,"
she'd murmur,
"*he*'s not there."


    2

Since spring, the hereafter
has been closer: the backyard
gardens thickening into bloom, Judas trees
smearing the yard with lavender,
constellations
gathered before us, as if heaven
had dredged up some order.
One by one, through the dry dusk,
the porch lights
come on, each swarmed by moths;
through the mosquitoey
light, a weak
moon is rising, and the hymn–
tremolo of Family Supper at church,
and the crickets'
meaningless amens:

how safe
my father seems tonight, how
absent—
cloistered, he bides his time, novice
of his dying: no elegy
reaches him and my hymns
filter slowly away through the stained glass.

# The Cursing of the Fig Tree

*after* Mark 11:12-23


While the apostles slept, or dully
gazed at the afternoon sky
desiring some woman of Galilee

or remembering the foam on a demon's mouth
or wondering how the damned thing would end,
Christ leaned for a while on a fig tree

and found himself strangely hungry,
touching it leaf by leaf
as if parting the lips of the dumb.

# Eurydice in Hades

The stink of gingko pods, welter of barbed leaves,
I remember

everything there. How smoke

wrapped and unwrapped the stripped trees,
mimicked, cloud by cloud, the whole sky,

torchlight on our faces, shadow and soot—

And pastures of sunflowers, swollen, grotesque, all bent
    toward the west
through the long-drawn summer afternoons

and the slow grazing of horses hunched in the fields—

I remember
how the dark-blue berries of viburnum

burst and smeared on my feet in the rainy night,

and hailstone storming the meadows
and the shock silver of olive leaves in the wind

and the purple puncture of the viper's bite on my heel—

Here the river arrives all day with its squalls,
barges scrape against docks

and the ferryman wards us back with his pole,

and the gnarling of the three dogs never subsides.
I spat out

the waters that would make me forget

when they captured me here
the first time,

remembering the smell

of mudbanks on a flooded river
above, the slap

of laundry against rock, and willows shimmering in
    the churning water.

I know my own face still, though the mirrors are empty,
though the huffed

prayers to the death god and processions of candlelit shadows

tempt me to drink, just once,
from the shallow river and wash out

those fields of asters and poppies, gullies

rushing and overflowing with rain: all
the mind I can't let go of, turning back

to witness again everything I'd never loved.

# Sweet Repeaters

*What part of a gambler's long-buried childhood is it
that forces its way to repetition in his obsession for play?*
—Sigmund Freud


In the hypnagogic
casino, I lean
to the clitter
of dice on the green
felt of the numbered table,
shoulder to shoulder with the loud
crowd crying

*All the hard ways*
while the shooter
spits in his fist,
bone-
rattle of die against die.
The stickwoman,
whose nametag says VENUS,

resumes her always–changing
chant, as the dealers
haul in the lost bets:
*Undershot,*
*Short by a dot,*
*Nothing sweeter*
*Than a repeater . . .*

—Something's
soothing in the patterned
repetition—hard
four and easy six and snake eyes two,

even
in the seven's rough
enchantment,

its power to wipe you out
or make you new.
It's not money that matters
but the measured
order, the hard
way through the fracas
on the table's

deranged and garish yellow and red—
then the pleasure
of reversion, the coming-again
of my number before the deadly 7
when the bet pays off its two for one.
Then there's consonance again, and I go back
to where that order

started, to the first
cadenced world where I held
number-shaped plastic blocks
in my fist (how sinuous
the six; how jagged, even then, the seven)
as I memorized
their names and shapes, the spells

an x or + could make them
cast.
Now the dice
trapped jerking in my palm
like a grasshopper,
now the rune of their rolling
over the Babel of $5 chips,

over painted dice on the felt
and the 4
forces its way to repetition
in the hypnagogic casino
and the red
stacks of chips, lit
by the roulette's distant neon wheel

double again,
and the Nooksack's
craps table hollers again, the shooter
having found at last his measure.

# Summer Mystagogia

*mystagogia: the period immediately following initiation into a mystery*

*. . . to discover an order as of*
*A season, to discover summer and know it*
—Wallace Stevens


I

4th of July: fireworks over Squalicum Harbor
hiss and vanish in a mist
strung down from the mountains.
The aquamarine
and viridian trails of fire
fizzle out in a muffle of cloud.
Only their last sparks
rip through, cut under,
while the white
we'd ordinarily ignore
is revealed as itself, shocked

open, lit for a moment from within.


2

The used
knowings of things
worn down: I stare
hard at this Thursday afternoon,
trying to make it surrender
whatever spirit underlies
its drought and incessant bloom:
quick shadow of gull
over surf-dreck, suck
of clamhole at low tide; in
the dilapidated boathouse

scribbled with *Life shits* and *Jesus*
*is Word made flesh* and
*Suck me off,*
no prayer burns the day into order,
nothing makes sense of the sensuous:
only tidewash again, and sundown, and gulls
snapping scraps of meat from burnt campfire sticks.


    3
The profligate
scum of wave, the hundred
crows in one poplar—
forty-seven-million sperm
on the fertility doctor's microscope slide,

his language *hysterosalpingogram,*
*intrauterine insemination,*
*an aggressive month for the ova—*

and, watching white globes
of cottonwood seed
glide through stabs of sun and fall
all over the mossed rock at my feet

I think of Jesus' parable
about the seed that died on rocky ground.

              Tell me
why seedpods are pouring
through a forest
that has not a single ungreen spot to fill.

    4
All day the Sound casts back its mess
of seal-head and seaweed-strangled driftlog
over stained, split rocks crushing morning glories.

Seagulls lined wing to wing
all along the tanker bridge.
Too much
of the brine smell, the sugar-ooze of fruit,
too much the world made up
by the senses, so
inhospitable to any order . . .

5

I used to live in a house without rooms
organized around a vodka bottle

none of us could find.
It was the invisible foundation

and everything we did
we did in response to it:

hidden deep in a clothes hamper, or
in a box of Kotex where my mother

thought we'd be ashamed to look,
it build the disordered house around itself,

arranged and rearranged
its own unchanged significance.

*Look at your mother, she's drunk*
my father

laughed, Mama slumped in the bathtub,
*she doesn't even know who you are . . .*

6

*A weakening of the sense of reality—*
that's what a mystic called sorrow,

saying joy is what we know when we know the real
for what it is. I know

a black litter of sea-pearl rose petals
in mud, under a dandelion's

half-blown stem . . .
There are days, like these, when faith

erodes a little, baring the root.

7

So no wonder tonight
the weeping silver birch
whips its fronds as though trying
to dislodge, onto the narcissus
and scarlet bleeding hearts,
all the dusklight it's hoarded.
No wonder the past seems
impregnable, and the moment of passage
into unambiguous dark
is deferred, twilight troubling its borders.
No wonder the world looks like
a place drained of wonder.

8

I live in a house that's stood for a hundred years
under a path in the sky where Arctic terns
shrill inland an hour after the ten o'clock dusk,
where gulls chase an eagle from the harbor down Victor Street.
I live in a house
built on the grounds of a syphilis clinic
so the doctor could escape his patients' cries—

On Sunday nights, the wind
(always on Sunday, no one can tell me why)
ravages this house,
once tore a door down the middle
and slung it across the yard.

Deep in August, the hollyhocks'
hundred blooms drag their stems to the ground.
A scraggle of yellowed tomato vine
offers up the one
ripe, distended fruit
that kills it.

And morning glory forces its way
through cracked floorboards
into the house.

I stand at the window, listening
in the scrape and crush of wind
for the orders I can barely make out anymore
of some magnitude, some
repossessing spirit: all

the muck and mystery
of summer, how
can I enter it.

# *Primavera*

She would have starved me out of the underworld
if she could have done it. He fed me
seeds that glistened red, he said
I needed at least that much
sustenance, reminder of earth. I needed
nothing but the hard realm of his body:
his ribs cold against my breast,
my tongue on the bones of his shoulders.
Now, dredged back, I can feel
blighted crops stir with an urge
to sprout. And I hate
this power of hers
over food and sex
she's forced on me, hate
being like her: sunflowers
droop and poppies wrinkle at my touch.
He's down there, watching, I know,
he must think
I belong to her inbreeding land again.
So I love to rake the fertile earth
to a compost of worms and beetles, rustle
the corn till I find a smear of slugs
on the stalks.
Just to spite her. And then feel the decayed
things burrow underneath, to the deeper
parts, where they belong,
and me. Above, stunted
tufts of olive trees; iris
and lobelia, and bullocks
straining their yokes through the deep
seed–rows; I straggle
through harrowed fields, remembering
how once the ground

unclosed for me. Now
my mother, in black veils still,
hovers over crocus and rose. She watches me
close as I walk from bush to bush,
suspicious,
afraid I'm not even the girl
she ravaged the crops to get back.
I think she longs for a new excuse
for her ritual mourning, the power
withheld nourishment
gave her. And in the starved,
bare flats of Hades, Dis
moves like her shadow, rousing
his own envious grief.
He can't stand not touching me
and he gazes through the furrows
as I squeeze the orange blooms
in my palms, spit,
tear the spears of hyacinth as quick
as she makes me
make them bloom, and fill—
just for him—my mudstained
apron to overflowing
with withering stalks of lilies.

# Ugly Ohio

*I know what we call it*
*Most of the time.*
*But I have my own song for it,*
*And sometimes, even today,*
*I call it beauty.*
—James Wright, *"Beautiful Ohio"*


I don't know why I live in Ohio,
where Stinking Creek
slithers past Hot Dog Heaven, and snowmelt
polishes the mashed, colorless weeds,
and locomotives
hunker past the beds of wasted orchards
and splintered windows of the Funeral Home.

Ice-stubs in mud, swaddle of mulch:
half-hearted unfreezing. Plum Creek's
skin of ice
salving its cuts
with its own melt—

April first, still the scab of the year.

     ∞

All I want
is to believe
in what pleasure
the flawed can give,

in what sunlight
can do to the wrinkled crusts
of oak leaves
that lasted all winter;

to thrill with the whipped
flag over Tappan Square
slapping its fifty stars,
with the quick sticks of the dead azaleas.

But I'm restless for Georgia's
figs and Cherokee roses, the pale pink
acid juice of the pomegranate,
tangle of lilac and lavender, and sweetgums
scalded to their roots in drench-rain and lightning.

∝

CLEAN DIRT
WANTED says a wet, scribbled sign
in a pasture by the dead-end highway,
strict rows of shadow and snow
laid like a plough's furrows.
I've never known *what* the bloated silos hold.

I could tell you
it's beautiful, this half-frozen muck,
stench of mudslides in sewer-bilge,
burnt-yellow factory smoke
over cowbarns,
but it would be, like the refuge of small talk,
a way of holding what's ugly at bay—
only a metaphor, and a lie,
metaphor meaning *to bear change.*
And nothing changes,
not even in April, in the flat,
streaked streets
of my alien Ohio,
except the white crumble
of last fall's
petrified dog turds
suddenly under my feet in Orchard Street's thaw.

# Idaho Compline

West, and west, the seeable world
urges, and you're drawn
there too, deviable: quarter-
lit over the half-snag
ponderosa pine, then
glinting under the silt
loam and shale, inside
fire-scarred root-wads
ripped out of eroded hills . . .

I have to squint
hard to find you
in the dusk shoving the visible lake
back to its far cove;
I have to squint hard
to witness
anything *but* you
in what dwindles and flames nearby

in the forest understory, where all
is infestation and fight:
crumble of humus,
worm and moss, cancerroot
and skullcap, dwarf
mistletoe deforming the firs
into a gnarl of witches' broom,
unhealable limb—

I glimpse you
rising off the burnt end
of Lost Man Trail, blear
as the drift of mist

into the gulch under Cougar Mountain
where I can't
reassemble you, running
my finger through woodpecker drills
over loose, bug-ridden bark.

There's nothing I want
you to give me:
I've quit asking
for anything but desire—
windflower and anemone in the nurselog's
woodrot.

Everything's gotten out,

Lord,
constellations
dropped like waterstriders on the lake—

What's to come
migrates here in its own time, unhinted-at,
self-divesting

        —as you divest
yourself again of all my goings-on,
even the words on my tongue,
the eye as it scans
the blacked-out lake
of Coeur d'Alene,
looking for some sign

of all this signlessness . . .

# Arcana Mundi

Everywhere doors stand open, everywhere
we dispose—with trouble—
of the familiar. A mockingbird
squawks and swoops to her nest in the tangled wild rose.
Strawberries hang, half ripe, hollowed by birds.
All day I've waited in vain for some message, some
accusation. Somewhere the sea turns
its salt wounds toward the sun. Somewhere
saints fall to their knees on carved marble. Here, clouds,
then stars, obscure the seven heavens.
The Boar flees through its haze, the Hunter moving low.
Cherry tree under their feet stripped of its fruit.
Look how the world whose mysteries I meant
to reveal to you, thing by thing,
lowers its seven veils and lets us stare.

# Advent: Snow Incantation

*Out of whose womb came the ice?*
*And the hoary frost of heaven, who hath gendered it?*
—Job 38:29


Somewhere in snowbanks black with car exhaust, chokeberry
flattened and dragging
icicles down to steaming sewers,
cut ice jangling dogwood limbs,

I mean to see
your spirit lay its shadow over the ice-light,

moon burnt-yellow and hard white over
hushed and rigid fields. Come
back to us, Father: this world

will be rectified. Tonight, I know,
you cross this field, white on white,
through the seized puddles and swamps of December,

a headless snowman flapping its scarves
in unbroken wind, while the roadside neon
delivers its message, word after word.

Can you hear
me, bodied as you are in the jagged chill, the freeze of slush
    and scattered berries?
Everything
rough and slick and shining
conceals you till I call
you back to this late fall, bedraggled
magnolias spotted with snow,
metallic scrape of shovels, tinkling of mournful tin bells.

All fall I have dreamed
of lying down with you,
openmouthed in a downpour of snow,
eyelid and tongue covered, my white
breath buried, and the heat of my flesh,

gone numb till I feel your chill
enter me at last: quick ash over slow ash—
And then I wake and it's over, startled sunlight,
    sudden loosening of ice,
the faraway gunning of cars
headed for work, frostburn
on my cheeks: the deep

recession into the ordinary

you order, hiding your face
inside the frozen drift of things, this shift
of your whited earth.

# Doxology

Let me laud you, God of salve and hurt,

begetter of all things
marred
and mercy-ridden—

This sprout of beggarweed, these lilac stalks
need say nothing: extolling
of scrub and vine. And even
the slackwater odor
of full gullies in drifts of sludge
attests to you—

There's nothing
the heavens haven't uttered
already in shudders
of animation more firm than words—

Flock of blackbirds over dull neon
in Thanksgiving's rainy dusk, rush
of wind through bare sweet
cherry, swelter of squirrels:

so little

abides,
so much recalls our turning
back toward you
*from whom all blessings flow*
endlessly away: magnificats
in the western smolder, praise
of what can't stay
unspeakable . . .

Let one
supplication cohere until I can utter it:

let what I call
out for come for me
sometimes,
and what I mean

and what it means for me,
touch—

# The Monologue of the Signified

What can dwell in your starved
syllable *I*,

so restless, so isolate, straining
upward so hard it wards
away the words on either side
with its limbs?

It hurts me
to speak like you, in these
rent syllables, always
scrambling from one crumbling word to the next—

What is meant

is meant to disintegrate;
with every scrape of consonant against vowel,

I empty myself, and you squander me.

&

I want
what thrums through the cords
of your throats
to utter *me* whole, want
to inhabit your vulgate:
glottis and tongue.

&

Do these labials
and repetitions
please you:
*lobelia,*

*bulimia,*
*landspit spar?* Vocables
are a form of starvation: it's no use
pretending you'd survive without me.
Your little verbs, when I abandon them,
are ravaged,
their ribs stabbing through.

    ∞

Names aren't numinous,
only the named
is.

    ∞

Even now you don't hear me, do you,

when I tell you
what it's like to be mute . . .

I can speak
in a way you can't even imagine,
monoglossia
far above all the anger of language.
But for you there are only these letters—
cowering, badly
camouflaged:
how they stagger
when I snatch them.

# from *A Mythic History of Alcoholism*

## *Denial: From My Diary, Age 10*

"Woke up.
Ate breakfast.
Went to school.
Came home.
Raked yard.
Jumped on pogo stick.
Made fire in back yard
and roasted hot dogs.
Daddy was drunk.
He kept hitting Mama.
Watched TV.
Went to bed."

## *From My Dream Diary, Age 10*

"We were primitive people.
Daddy had to hunt for our food.
When he gave me fish eggs
to eat, snakes
kept hatching out of them."

## *Narcissus*

After work every day, Daddy
would stir his drinks over the sink,
stare for an hour
into the bathroom mirror,
watching himself get drunk
enough to come out for supper.

## The Sacrifice of Isaac

The woodcutter's axe
thumping far away, somehow
comforting,

Hansel
hunched in the dead leaves,
calling *Father* . . .

But he found
only a branch tied to a withered tree
beating in the wind.

When he got home:
*Wicked children,*
*why did you sleep so long in the forest?*

## Watching Mama for Signs of Drinking After Daddy Died

Forty nights without rain:
Noah walked the mountain, stepping
suspicious on still-spongy ground, watching
doves drop twigs from their mouths,
gash of rainbow across the half-black sky.

## The Serpent Beguiled Me

*I can't live with your daddy*
*unless I have a little*
*something to drink,*

Mama said, neck
splotched with bruises, pouring
them both another whiskey.

After he died: *I can't*
*live without your daddy,* clutching
her fifth of vodka
as she stood

over the hissing iron, crying.

## Leaving Childhood

It never stays
far enough away: an accidental
click of the ruby slippers, and everything
grays and grains into Kansas
again, the blown-away house
restored, pitchfork
still stuck in the dirt, and everyplace
I turn looks, uncannily,
like home . . .

## Humpty Dumpty

Isis is reassembling Osiris again:
her papyrus boat
poling through the marshes
because the putting-back-together is never done—
So: map the bottle's daily
changing hiding place:
trashcan, fireplace, cookie jar, commode.

Pour out what's left of the whiskey
when they've passed out and the liquor stores are closed.
Record your father's
rages, leave the tape
on the kitchen table at breakfast.
Tell your neighbors
he's only gathering firewood
when he stalks the yard
with a hatchet, Mama
locked hiding in the car. Isis
is gathering from the reeds of the Nile
a basket, an arm, a tongue. The reassembly's
always going on: hold
together the cracked
mask of myth, its
pieces sharp and useless over your face.

## Elegy: Narcissus and Echo

Narcissus is drowned, and Echo

helpless not to repeat
his last words: *O darling boy*
*whose love was my undoing;*

helpless
not to repeat
chugged liquor, delirium tremens,
the locked
psychiatric ward,

then the grave plot

by the Ocmulgee.
Twice in five years, I walked there,
in black, watching
the world stir, dulled,
distorted on the river's skin—

*Alas*, Narcissus sighed, bending
to drink from that longed-for image,
that self-in-concentric-
waves the drinking could never reach,

and Echo, in pity, was able
to answer
with her own voice, her own
wasting-away
after him, *Alas*.

# After an Adoration

They don't know what to do now they're here, leaning

on the crumbling beam of a manger
bisected by light

among oxen and asses, a carpenter's
tools, scrub

hills receding into blurred ruins.
Into each adoration, some peculiar

disillusion intrudes: always
someone in the crowd of pilgrims

averts his eyes from the Christ child
and glares accusingly outward

as though the arrival
had satisfied nothing. Only

the haloes redeem
the squalid scene: beasts'

breaths fuming in starlight,
barnfowl and peacocks flocked in the crossbeams.

One wise man's
mind has begun to go, and he stares

at some evil he believes
has followed him

the whole way, lodged now
in the shadowed rafters of this shed. Not

one of them could tell you what
all their longing

has accomplished: they're left
to stare into a wooden shack

where the cold
child whimpers and its mother

flails her arms in her sleep. After
an adoration, the shock

of how much remains
unrevealed; so awkwardly

the magi kneel
in the pawed dirt

littered with gold, beseeching the helpless savior.

# Sleeping in Santo Spirito

Shut out
of Masaccio's chapel where I'd tried
three times to see Eve and Adam

hunted by the angel, hiding
their genitals and eyes,
this afternoon I went instead

to sleep in the damp heat
of Santo Spirito. I watched
a priest in a black cassock,

swinging his silver censer, mount
the high altar to the Host
suspended among gold

to remake it into flesh.
Filthy, half-asleep, I thought
how the Gnostics wore black

to grieve the soul's
imprisonment in the flesh.
I watched him

consecrate and crack
the brittle tablet, dissolving it
bit by bit on his tongue, mumbling

*Corpo di Cristo* . . . Hunched
low in my seat at the dim
edge of the transept, I fell

asleep as the congregation
rose in communion, their hymn
resounding foreign and hollow

across the vaulted glass.
My clothes were foul
with sweat; I'd walked

miles to see the Expulsion, and stood
spent before the scaffolded chapel, its door
draped with a cartoon of the two

tormented figures. Aching
all over, I saw
that shut chapel again as I breathed

the holy smoke
of Santo Spirito, the votive
candles still burning behind my eyes. The black

back wings of the stone angel
smeared into sleep, with the wooden
donation boxes for the souls

of Purgatory, only
the faraway incantations of the Mass
holding me up.

I woke to a black-cloaked monk
staring me down, his harsh
eyes accusing me of sickness

or sacrilege: slouched
over a dim pew
carved with gnarled gargoyles, I was caught

half-asleep in the house of the Holy Ghost.

# A Dogwood Tree in a Country Graveyard, at Easter

*(According to legend, Christ was crucified on the wood of a dogwood tree.)*

The blessing,
if it were visible,
would resemble a single bloom:
small white blister in the sun.

Pure except
for an imperfect umber border,
this flower ragged-eared and bleeding,
like a ghostly X, rood for spring.

In the churchyard surrounded by graves
this dogwood skulks along the walls
and shadows each blade of grass.

Watch how it carries its blossoms,
all four corners held square at the sky,
as if it knew its legend,
how something big was released from pain . . .

&infin;

This pale April, the branches
fork just where the wrists went suddenly limp
and the stem breaks into a swollen blossom,

a blur of what's happening downfield:
the creek forcing a hollow through dandelion,
thicket of milkweed dressing the tombs.

The last buds, arranged for emergence,
nodding—at whomever—their
half-hearted offer.

✖

A leaf glitters at sundown.
White laundry stirs in the dull wind.
The people here aren't mourning anything.

✖

Only a detail,
camellias gone white by the wooden house
nearest the churchyard.

A woman's been dead there awhile.
Horses stand by the back porch
like a few words of sympathy.

There's only
the shadow of a steeple on wet grass,
annunciations of crickets at twilight.

On Mother's Day, in May, the family
will cross the pasture wearing camellias,
pale white for the death of a mother.

✖

Easter Sunday. 11 o'clock
and the whole town arrives,
hymnbooks opened, matches struck,
sunlight drifting in through the praying faces.

And already another year renounced:
flashes of silver and candles,
music rising as if to heaven
and everyone bending to pray in the faint light:

and white petals of dogwood falling like grace
across the stained windows, the undistinguished graves.

# Ultrasound

*The Loneliness One dare not sound*—Emily Dickinson

I

Halloween, and we flew
toward my grandfather's deathbed
in Briarwood Convalescent, in Atlanta,
while the ticket agents, in holiday
skeleton suits, giggled.

That morning, after the phone call, the Puget Sound
rose and spat in its mist
behind the traintracks and smokestacks
of Georgia Pacific, as Suzanne and I
walked by the seawall (she bearing
for eight weeks a child he'd never see now),
watching the rain reswelling the Sound,
the water reverting to its first, shapeless form—

And no one could read the ultrasound
pictures two days later,
after his funeral on the Day of the Dead,
after the casket
scraping its metal:
through a swarm of static
three black, interlocked
circles under a mass of cyst—
*twins*, the doctors guessed, or *triplets*
or *molar pregnancy:* the fetuses
feeding as triple tumors on the uterine wall—

*I'll tell you what I'm not seeing,*
the doctor said,
*I'm not seeing any heartbeats.*

2

In our minds we filled them in
as they would have been:
with their arms—the pregnancy book said—only as long as
    exclamation points,
with their lung buds and their tongues,
already-beating hearts
migrating into the sealing flesh of their chests,
with their bodies weighing less than a thirtieth of an ounce
we imagined them taking hold,
primitive, physical, quickening, ours.


3

In the newspaper that week, a photograph
of the vicinity of a black hole:
three swirls of black

in an X of caught dust: inescapable
turning-inward, decreation
of matter and light.
It swirls at the center of the galaxy
and nothing from there comes back.


4

*Nothing which exists*, says Simone Weil,
*is absolutely worthy of love;*
*we must therefore love that which does not exist.*

Decreated ones,

you who turn back from matter,
from the Sound held on the horizon
by the freeway and a coiled black smudge of mountain clouds,

who reveal yourselves as empty
black marks on a photo strip, the dumb
hum of life-machines—

you, my grandfather, who
shouted, stripped to your diapers, near the end
*I'm in the middle of something*
*but I don't know what I'm in the middle of,*

I'll stay here, in the middle,
in the fifteen-hour nights before the solstice,
in the season of a sacred birth,
where the apple tree bears up its three weak leaves,
where you of ninety years, and you of nine weeks, vanish
and the earth goes on bearing
too much that isn't you:
always too much, and always
this helpless wanting something
different—

                              —wanting to witness
a voice above words, beyond sound,
that would read
this strip of loss, these
pictures of what isn't there
and sound for me the washed, gray
gash of the harbor,
black sacs in static haze,
mudblack trench of my grandfather's grave,
and fill in for a moment

whatever is gone,
the Sound always lost in cold, blown fog.

# Before Thanksgiving

Abundant deprivation,
glossolalia
of hail on windows, the splintered
ice crust of the roadside muck:

I take names
of things that remain—
stinkhorn rising over dead sweet basil,
the roses' chokehold, still, on the frozen summerhouse.

# Going Home to Georgia

Beyond the pawn shops and tattoo parlors and Tofu House
of Atlanta, the highway drones
out to the squat, clipped peach trees
in pink and green flower
and the roadside doublewide
V.I.P. Massage Parlor
("Truckers Welcome")
and the purple
quilts of Leonardo's *Last Supper*
flapping in the March wind, by the gargoyles
and lawn gnomes
and tin-roofed shacks
and crosses scrawled with warnings of hellfire
and buzzards

wheeling low. I remember, suddenly, Orvieto—
how, in Signorelli's fresco
of the torments of the damned, the noose
by which a devil strangles a young woman
has disappeared, worn down
by centuries on the church wall. And he yanks,

still, at the nothing between them,
his green foot pressed to her temple,
while the green- and pink-winged angels
stand arrogant over the scene, beating back
the rising damned,
barely glancing at the horrors below.

There's enough we can see
to choke us
in the crumbling chimneys and steeples
in the half-rain, half-sun
of this late afternoon,
the Buford Highway Body Shop's
billboard: "Jesus Christ
is the way, truth, and light. Free

estimates . . ."

—I've come back to Macon for the first time
in years, old smell of stagnating
water and honeysuckle blent
through what's left of Baconsfield Park.
Willed by a Confederate general
for the "enjoyment of white women and children,"
it's sold now
by Supreme Court order and sporting
McDonald's and condos surrounding
the swampy, magnolia-shadowed pond
where I, a white child, gathered
salamanders with my father
twenty-six years ago.

Now the graves of my parents
lie abandoned, side by side,
with five years separating their last days,
the unseeable torments of the drunk
that drove them both to want to lie
down here before their time.
I've come back with what I've been able
to shore against their dread,
what things might suffice to heal
this world without losing it: rainy
sunlight over Rose Hill, miles
of pool halls and wrecked Plymouths, mounds
of hubcaps and inner tubes, wild
iris and cabbage palm and stakes of crosses—for the first
time since they died I can breathe
the sweet, soiled air
of this swampy burying ground
again and answer them both

it's enough, and enough, the stuff of this world.

# The Conceiving

*Invisible are all beings before birth and after death invisible again;*
*they are seen between two unseens. Why in this truth find sorrow?*
—The Bhagavad–Gita

I

What's this exhaustion, breath
after breath after breath, this turning–

inward to escape
from smaller and smaller

talk? I have always wanted to be
anonymous, unbidden into speech,

withdrawn
into what remnant of the spirit's

left in me,
and there I find you,

uncreated, in that poverty of the senses
where you stay,

prefoetal and invisible and blind.
If I make us a haven

here inside,
hypostasis of father and child,

not physical yet, not real,
will you let me lead you back

to earth someday, will you forgive
what avarice makes us make you

come alive? This transubstantiation
would give you

a life like ours, so glutted
with things I sometimes make my way

out of it awhile
to rest in your stripped landscape; going out,

I cut a swath
from here to there, a clearing

by which someday you'll find your own way in.

2

Here at the Cinque Terre—
the five earths—
we wait for you
in raw, unmediated places, an earth
almost too physical to endure:
surfspume into algae-colored grottoes of cloven stone,
octopus-tendrilled
cactuses crawling off sea cliffs,
here where the soul's
impossible to tell
from the objects of its appetite:
burnt crusts of bread, strips
of black-roasted red peppers, oozing their oil:

five earths, five senses, what veils and seals to tear . . .

3

Look at the gulls stunned over downbent sea-pines
and the schooners anchored in the noon–still of the bay
and the lighthouse waiting, withholding
its timed
shocks—

It's a place
with a stasis of its own,
and flux as well: smell,
all at once, these rosemary sprigs
on turning skewers of chicken,
and tufts of honeysuckle,
and the salt
sea—

Then beg creation to admit you,
the way roots
that have cracked a stone wall
grow thick, sealing the fissure.

4

Untethered one, if you dare
enter this place of appetite
with nothing but sleep and prayer
to take you back,

we'll hold you
and recite you the new world's things:
sienna, magenta, ivory,
woodgrain and grain of stone,
shrunk soap,
heaped peaches, exultation
of bells—

Such profusion
you'll watch recede from you,
richer and more splendid as it goes,
hour after hour,

sandspit and grave.

    5
This bodily life: it costs
distance, and diminishment,

wave after wave raised from a lost disturbance,
some mid-ocean squall

that gave them birth.
But see them

arrive here where slate's
layered over limestone,

seagrass and slime,
where the Gulf

of Paradise floods the land's hollows.
It's labor

and a kind of worship to let creation
enter through the senses

in all its defective
splurge: poppies on mulepaths,

teal glut of the surf
the instant before it breaks: come bear

witness with us, child, among
the things that come and overwhelm us and vanish again.

# EXTREMITIES

from *Signs and Abominations* (2000)

*forerunner—*

# What Did You Come to See

*Jesus began to say unto the multitudes concerning John, What*
*went ye out into the wilderness to see? A reed shaken with*
*the wind? . . . But what went ye out for to see? A prophet?*
*Yea, I say unto you, and more than a prophet.*
—Matthew 11: 7-9

There's always something sepulchral
John the Baptist wants us to see, something
that will ravish us more than he will—

see how he gestures (forerunner)
toward the timeless, sacred scene,
leading, if you follow him, the eye

away from his muscles and camel-hair rags,
hung pelts of his robe, the black wilderness skin—
and the corrected,

redirected gaze
moves over the canvas, to the Virgin
and Corpse with arrow-

ridden, ghastly saints,
ageless, toothed
cleavers stabbed inside their haloes.

The pointing Baptist is always there
only not to be there, to exempt
himself from the scene of redemption

so he glares straight-on and his finger
begs us not to look at *him*,
which makes me gaze all the harder

at his honeycomb and locusts, his thin
reed cross: What did you come
to see, a reed

shaken in the wind? Icon
of not looking, of returning the gaze
to what lies far beyond the phenomenal—

So, on the highway to San Sepolcro,
roadsigns for miles proclaimed
PREGNANT MADONNA, NEXT EXIT—

Madonna del Parto, in her roadside shrine, restored,
but we still missed the exit, counting
whores, in gold lamé, red

leotards, waving at truckers,
while the signs
pointed, insistent: Piero

della Francesca's Madonna
del Parto, exit, exit . . .
There's always something incongruous

the world wants us to see, pointing
away from Christ's gestation
to the dairy truck

screeched into gravel-ruts,
the prostitute's leotard split open at the crotch
as she runs to meet it, and the gaze

redirects itself, refocuses, and the sacred
and its restored
depictions

blur.

∞

In Palma Giovane's self-portrait,
he's so mixed in with his scene
of Transfiguration, you can hardly tell

who's the painter, who apostles and saints
with their arms cast out in astonishment
at the Christ blasted off into light:

except that *he* holds the splattered brush,
and so paints his own way in
even as we watch, transfiguring

his life to a scene of the holy:
how should we direct our gaze? to the painter, to Christ,
to the witnesses cowering from the blare

of light? Or look back
from what we can bear to see
to the sign of what we can't,

apostle gone blind from the sight. Icon
of unseeable splendor: what
*did* we come to see? A foppish

man in stole and beret, who's stared
for four hundred years, believing
his own brushstrokes could grant him entry to that Kingdom—

Not like the Baptist, all
beast-skin and exposed muscle, no sign
of his martyrdom, no severed head

—emplattered—to show us, who stands
in a wilderness of his own making,
pointing away.

I stared at his finger
crooked toward the business of the cross,
clumped vein over bone in the twisted wrist,

and barely glanced toward Calvary.
Signs, abominations:
it's always the diversion

that attracts me,
what doesn't mean to be seen that I need
to stare down, until it's just dried

pigment on a canvas, ground
lapis lazuli, ultramarine, daubed
strokes in eggwash and squirrel-hair,

something wholly of its own time (truckstop, split
leotard) of which
it keeps telling us: Don't look.

# Negatives of O'Connor and Serrano

*. . . writers who see by the light of their Christian faith will have,
in these times, the sharpest eyes for the grotesque, for the perverse,
for the unacceptable.*
—Flannery O'Connor

*God created the body for a reason, and we were meant to exploit it.*
—Andres Serrano

*O one, o none, o no one, o you:*
*Where did the way lead when it led nowhere?*
—Paul Celan

### NEGATIVE 1

Andres Serrano would jack off on Jesus

(the congressman said)
if the NEA would pay him to do it—

*What this Serrano fellow did,*
*he filled a bottle with his own urine*
*and stuck a crucifix down there,*

*he is not an artist, he is a jerk—*

—He jerks off
in the air, and photographs
his semen's fretted
transit through space, *Ejaculate*

*in Trajectory,* abjected seed. What leaves
the body. It's substance
he wants, not representation:
blood and cum, milk and Christ, submersible
icons. Black spume all around the Last Supper.
In O'Connor's *bleeding, stinking, mad*

*shadow of Jesus,* cibachrome
Pieta in cow's blood, Jesus seethed in piss—

Strip of negatives, images
stripped down to their substance, stripped of their light.

NEGATIVE 2

*No truth,* shouts Hazel Moates, *No truth behind all truths is what I
    preach . . .*

Stains of menstruation
Serrano preaches: used Maxi-pads, cratered landscape of blood.
Plotinus calls the physical world
the font of all defilements and confusions. It's unbodying
we want, *un*knowing, to know a God
*luminous, incomprehensible*

*(Nor is He body, nor has He form or shape),*
the Negative Way to That
Which transcends all affirmation—

Or so says Pseudo-Dionysius.
Jin, in his baby backpack, belly-laughs
at the woman's strap-on dildo
in Serrano's *History of Sex,* already, at six months, knowing
incongruity of breasts and cock—

Via negativa, radical denial:
to strip from what we say of God all that He is not
*(Neither has He power, nor is He power, nor light)—*

what's left's
shriveled, inchoate, known

incongruity of numinous substance and world . . .

84

## NEGATIVE 3

**morgue Klux Serrano menstrual piss**

the Internet tells me. Refined
search terms littering the bottom of the screen. Unholy
scat. Unbodying
quest: *Show me where your wooden leg
joins on.* Serrano's
bloodscapes, Hazel Moates'
barbed wire and lime-burnt eyes.

Evil, I read, is nothing

but the tendency of things toward nothingness—
In a creation God made good, iniquity
must be like the zero, a hollow
that in multiplication reduces
everything to itself.

And so this apophasis, this
orbiting of the 0:
We have to approach supernatural grace
negatively, O'Connor says
(*Grace would have to be violent to compete with the evil*

*I can make concrete),* have to show where it's not, not where it
      is, tracing
the fretted tracks its long trajectory leaves.

## NEGATIVE 4

Not where it is. In the Children's Crusade, 10,000 boys
straggled from France toward the Holy Land
(censers, wax candles, oriflammes),
chanting prayers for the Mediterranean

to dry up and let them cross.
At each walled hilltown outside Paris,
they pointed and cried, Is that Jerusalem?
Is that Jerusalem, the profaned

holy land just across the walled-off square,
is *that* Jerusalem, the plastic
Pope smeared with menstrual blood,
tabooed. Unbodying

debodied One, is that
Jerusalem, the chill
sea-wave rushing against those children's feet?
Or the seven

rotted ships that wrecked
halfway to Palestine
on San Pietro, the boy-
pilgrims' bodies washed, eternally

undecomposing, to that shore?

## NEGATIVE 5

In Serrano's *Auto-Erotic*, the model
licks his own cock,
face lurid in burnt-red light, cheeks
hollowing to suck himself harder—

(*I don't need no hep*, says the Misfit,
*I'm doing alright by myself*)

Self-love, the concupiscent
tongue, cockhead's wet tip:

ache of the torso's contortion,
misfit
of self to self.

Unbodying quest,
for substance: *Love Him,*
Meister Eckhart preaches, *as He is: a not-God,*
*a not-Person, a not-spirit, a not-image—*

The Bible case
crammed with condoms

and a wooden leg. *Deformed*
*I,* Augustine says, *plunging*
*amid those fair forms*
*which Thou hast made—*

NEGATIVE 6

Amid the fair forms, Serrano's
plexiglas Cross full of blood,
O'Connor's hermaphrodite, in its tent,
*God made me*

*thisaway, I don't*
*dispute hit—*

I don't dispute it, the secret,
the secreted
(blood, choler, phlegm, bile),
all things the flesh
can't keep, can't keep

hidden. All
defilements, all confusions:
crucifix lopsided on a mound of chicken hearts,
pickled brains floating in pedestalled vials.
Lashed Christ, tattooed into Parker's back, *haphazard*

*and botched.* Super–
Essential Darkness, God is beyond
any name we can give Him, any image

that would show Him, Dionysius tells us, *beyond*
*all affirmation, all negation . . .*

NEGATIVE 7

Monica Lewinsky's
blue semen-stained dress, seized
for DNA tests.
There are no curtains
in the Oval Office.
Newt Gingrich: "Eatin' ain't cheatin'."
*For the purposes of these depositions,*
*an act of sexual congress shall mean*
*any and all genital contact.*
Ed Bradley, on primetime TV:
"When the President placed your hand
on his genitals, was he *aroused*?"
Meanwhile, the plexiglas Popemobile
in Havana. Mass in Che Guevara's square.
Eight-story banner of Christ. Pamphlets
to the people: *The Pope*
*is not a politician, not a tourist, not*
*a magic remedy.* The press'
departure from Cuba to cover the semen spot,
dress hauled off and scrutinized
thread by thread, like the Holy Shroud. Was He aroused.

## NEGATIVE 8

White Christ
purified in a vat of milk.
Hazel Moates: *One Jesus is as bad as another.*

Negatives, darkened texts,
reversed icons, blotched, from which
the representational illusion proceeds, print, and print—

*Of neither the things that are, nor of the things that are not*

From his butcher on 38th, Serrano
hauls back to the studio his gallons of blood

*Neither does He live, nor is He life*

In a dream, even books
are mortal: crusted
tumors on their pages, leeching
fleshwounds on their covers

*Neither can reason attain to Him, nor name Him, nor know Him*

(Serrano's
slammed and jeweled cathedral gates)

Hazel Moates: *Where
has the blood you think
you been redeemed by*

*touched you?*

# Hermetic Diary

I

     . . . As if lyric
should overtake story, world
shrunken back to a hungering

cry,
its votive-candle words
sputtering their O and their O . . .

Relit, today, at dawn. Invisible
vestibule, where you wait.

Unapproachable
child, when
will you come to us, and on

what plane?

2

Rose moss over rain-garish
brick. As if sequence
should reassert itself
(dim sum, dinner at Lumiere, stared-
down and unringing
phone),
so that things might proceed

into time. So that time
might be no more.

3
Substitutive,

unbegotten:
by Christ's wounds, the five
stigmata,

knot–roses, inward–
gone.

Assisi earthquake: cracked
Cimabue. St. Peter, in crumbled
plaster, unhealable,
healing
the possessed.

The possessive. Who wait. Streaks
of cirrostratus, pulp mill
odor of sopped wood through the window.

Supplicative
barred crib.

Call,
response. I call
you, child, not-yet

known:
blister–
rose the dusk sky

keeps twisting


*—for Jin: waiting for his adoption*

# Hermetic Self-Portrait

*avoiding likeness and autobiographic gesture*

I

Mid-gut
of the imago, the instars'
moults. And the grasshopper
becomes a burden. In the suburbs, cicadas
seethe from the ground
every seventeen years

(forty thousand from the roots
of one tree)
to breed, and die.
And the empty skins
crackle everywhere underfoot,
tiny golden shells
hung on every surface.

Slough of the tough
carapace, dark thorax, red
front-margin of the wings
pumped full of juice.

Shriek. The ribbed
snaredrums of their abdomens—
the grackles are terrified
by their buzz-saw
song, the neighbors deafened by it . . .

Where am I
in this

emergence—

2

Ground punctured with exit holes.
Convulsive
split of the husk: bulbous
eyes, and greasy wings—

This coming
out of oneself, for good, this
leaving hundreds of eggs behind—

This leaving
a finished body behind.

Can a man bear a child,
Jeremiah asks,
the resurrection nymph's

disturbance-squawk . . .

3

Can a man *bear*

a child. *Mutare*, to change. From which comes
*moult*. Their music-making
is a mating call, hollow
longing sound like *pharaoh, pharaoh*—

On my parents' tombstone, a dying cicada.
Having bred. It crawled up my pantsleg
when I touched it, the pitched

squeal of its brood around us—

No bouquet
laid down. I'm all out of *white* roses,
the florist had said,
I'm all out of *red* roses, too,
I don't have a single carnation left,

to be honest with you,
I'm plumb out of *every* kind of flower,

I don't even know why I'm here . . .

    4
Foghorn
as the music
of insomnia, sounding

all night from the whited-
out harbor
a mile away.

Mist in the nursery window,
three balloons tethered
to the new crib.

In the hall outside,
I stroke my mother's hair,
sealed into her still-life's

oilpaint, stray black S
through the pink carnation,
seventeen years

she's been gone . . . Warning
of the foghorn's hollow
four-second moan,

stilled music
of insomnia, means
of finding ground.

5

So let me come
out of myself, a synchronous
burrowing out of the earth:

black S, still
life, crib's
white balloons, stridulous

cry, *long*
*deep tones in fog or darkness,*
pink painted carnation, seventeenth

year in this emergence. I make the sign
of the cross
over the two names on the grave,

over the belly-up cicada—then its wings
flapping wild in my face, my glasses
knocked off—

6

Brood. To tell you the truth,
I'm plumb
out of incarnation,
crunched shells
of cicadas, empty
chitinous husks, the nymphs
tunneling into the loam, for a dormant
life.

Long wait
while the nursery fills
with hand–me–downs, with gifts

(Ground littered with fallen bodies, stiffened
wings)—

Staring
at the fog-window,
drag of white, half-visible balloons,

drag of scraggled
lines across the page:

I don't even know
why *I'm* here.

# Mutating Villanelle

Because God wants us to have indefinite life, like Him,
Richard Seed intends to electroshock an egg
to implant his image and likeness into Gloria, his wife

    (to implant into Gloria, his menopausal wife, his shocked
        image and likeness)

after inducing quiescence in its nucleus (moon-pause)
so his DNA might nest there and live forever,
cloned, and cloned, indefinite life God wants us to have, like Him.

Enucleated oocyte, like the lamb-clone Dolly's.
Lamb of God, who takes away the sins of the world
(implanted sin, aboriginal, in the image and likeness of God,
    Gloria

in excelsis Deo) . . . *Heaven forbid,*
his ex-wife said, *I wouldn't trust him to breed a tadpole.*
God wants us like Him, in His image, after His likeness, seed

      (having shed "indefinite"
         having shocked into fusion the two mutating refrains)

fallen on fertilized ground. Nucleus hollowed, egg
shocked into taking the alien
cell into its image and likeness, glorious implantation.

                (lamb-
                clone, 237
                grotesque miscarriages
                before it was born)

*Lamb of God, you take away* our imperfections,
through manipulation of the flawed genes.
Because God wants us to be like Him, indefinite
        (because God wants us,
        wants us clones of Him)
how soon will the womb of Gloria be implanted (*What rough beast*)
    with the image and likeness of seed . . .


        (Enucleated
        iambs, perfectible
        refrains [to hold oneself
        back, forbear],
        imperfectible rhymes
        [glory/story, likeness/
        Loch Ness]:
        grotesque
        miscarriage
                    indefinite
                    likeness,
        glory, electroshock, tadpole, rough beast, seed)


how soon will the womb of Gloria be implanted (*Hail, O
        favored one, the Lord is with thee*) with the image and likeness
        (fore-born) of Seed . . .

# Errata Mystagogia

*Summer Mystagogia, 1996 Colorado Prize for Poetry*

There, in the misprints and vacant
pages, garbled
syntax of the proofreaders' spoils,

even the word *disfiguring* disfigured,
in the trail of twelve misspellings,
where adjectives cling to the wrong
nouns (*woodwasps*
instead of *dogwoods*
made pink),

I track the unfixable

everywhere, its slippery
letters, lessons
no one wants to know how to learn.

Where Augustine poses his question
so emphatically
it takes *two* question marks
to get it right:
*All these lovely but mutable*
*things, who has made them*
*but Beauty immutable??*

This mutable
book, its muted
voice, goes out to its warehouses and bookshops
with three pages gone,
second half of "The Reliquary Book"
(beginning "its passages
unmovably bound")

left blank, bound—
by the printwheels' skip—
to oblivion.
So I write this
errata sheet
for the uncorrectable proof
of all things: initiation
into the half-

hearted and bungled, *jug*
become *jog, beaks*
transfigured to *breaks,*
the *aggrsseive month for the ova,*
ellipses
inserted in the middle of a word
as though the lacuna
of language
couldn't help but bleed through . . .

*If Wallace Stevens had won the Colorado Prize,*

a friend tells me, *we'd be reading
"Anecdote of the Jog . . ."*

October, no apology from the editor,
no answer at all, word
of a relative
with water surrounding her heart, rain
dribbling from a birdbath where hollyhocks
shed the last of their pink
(woodwasps? erratum: blooms)

over a gash in the ground where a shallow-
rooted forsythia collapsed in a squall—

On the news, the usual
botch: Scrub of clearcut hills, hacked
groves of juniper and fir, cheery
senator posed over the saplings:
READY FOR HARVEST IN 2035—

Then a man
with a hatchet
left permanently in his head, its blade
too close to the brain

to remove.
*The book*
*broken*

in a mutable world, errata
inserted in the place of every page.


—*for David Milofsky*

# from *Spiritual Alphabet in Midsummer*

*The various states of soul in a man must be like the letters in a dictionary,*
*some of which are powerfully and voluminously developed, others having*
*only a few words under them—but the soul must have a complete alphabet.*
—Søren Kierkegaard, in his diary


## A

This is the finger of God:

gnat-swarm in fruitbowl, torn
flap of plumskin
riddled with them, blackberry
vinegar, in its open decanter,
thick with swimming gnats—

I walk through the house, laughing
lines from Exodus (I'm teaching
the Bible as Literature
for extra money): *There*
*came gnats*
*on man and beast, all the dust*
*of the earth became gnats,*
*and the magicians said,*

*This is the finger of God . . .*

Hyssop dipped in lamb's blood,
hail and fire in thunder, Raid
Flying Insect Killer's
pillar of cloud over the stove, *I will smite*
*the land of Egypt*—

Jehovah's Witness once at the door,
fat hellflames lapping at the *Watchtower* cover:
*Lotsa people they think Hell*
*is hot—,*
*but Hell's not hot, it's not, it's not . . .*

Merciful
God, of temperate
Hell, harden
our hearts this summer, so that signs
and wonders

may be multiplied—
Deadly
nightshade twined around the raspberry canes—
We lick
raspberry juice
from each other's fingers. Black
vinegar swirling down the disposal, compost
bin's sweet reek of fruit,

sprayed gnats dropped on the microwave,
finger of God
on everything, its

smudged, unmistakable print.

## B

In the year of our Lord one thousand
three hundred and seventy-three,
Julian of Norwich, *living*
*in this mortal flesh,*
felt her spiritual eyes slip open

and she gazed on Christ
enthroned inside her
(*a delectable and restful sight*)

serene, implacable, eternally
holding court there
as if her soul *were a kingdom*
*and a fine city.*

Monday, in a dream, mine
was laid bare: hushed
attic room, unfinished, hot,

abandoned window fan's rusted blades
blocking the crawlspace
I kept crawling through,

and frizzled wires
at the end of each passage
hissed and sizzled, sputtering
fire—

*And soon afterwards all was hidden*
*and I saw no more.*

# C

To learn the spirit's alphabet, its spells

of heat and freezing,
I have to find my way beyond the vowels,

mellifluous containers of desire:
the real work waits in the consonants,
oilslick along the inside of the drum,

smirched smell of what's not usable, not saved.

*The self says, I am,*
says Roethke,
*the heart says, I am less,*
*the spirit says, You are nothing.*

To be nothing, in summer, when sweetpeas
wind strangling around their stick,
when my hollyhocks lift their stalks—
ladder-spoked with pink blooms—as high as the roof

(My place in the world
that is not my place—)

When everything stakes and stakes
its extravagant
claim to being

through rarer and more complicated forms of beauty.

To be nothing, and to want to be that,
diminished and joyed in diminishment,

like the catarrhal
rasp of the poppy's seedpods

hollowed on cracked stems and spewing
thousands of invisible

seeds on the wind that distributes
also their long, deceptive

death-rattle from the dry stalks . . .

# D

*The whole of existence*

*frightens me,*
Kierkegaard wrote in his diary,
*from the smallest*
*fly to the mystery*
*of the Incarnation . . .*

So Serrano's *Piss Christ:* divinity
suspended in human

waste, the nailed body bubbling
down through urine-filtered, mystic

gold-red light,
Incarnation as willed submersion

in what even the flesh rejects—
Kafka's diary: *the joy*

*again of imagining*
*a knife twisted in my heart . . .*

# F

O inhabitant of the Earth,

August melancholia, insomnia, dog days
hazed in gray. Tetris
at 3 a.m., in between
Genesis chapters in *God: A Biography*—
in both, the compulsive
filling-up of the empty. Anhedonic
god, domesticated

in his desert tent, sniffing the wind
for the scent of burnt meat—

His obsession with us, His spirit-life
—rage, wrath, jealousy, vengeance,
displeasure and pride,

never rejoicing—*God does not rejoice* . . .
Who turned to make
no other world,
mad to remain in this one, desert and flood—

I wonder
what He wants from me now,
3 a.m., up thinking
how useless I am, how dull, reading
*I will smelt away your dross.*

—Pleasureless

Lord of Hosts, what remorse, what envy,
stirs in You now,
as in me,

what scrutiny by the dim nightlamp?

## I

*How are the dead raised, with what*
*body do they come?:*

David Gee has willed his skin
to a tattoo artist, all
seventeen square feet of it, in magenta

and pink and brown
serpents and bulls and bats

($33,000 worth of tattoos,
500 hours under the humming knife)

with the one stipulation that it be stripped,
tanned, and permanently displayed

*So that people continue to see me after I'm dead—*

—St. Bartholomew,
in the Last Judgment,
brandishes a knife and trails his flayed skin

on which Michelangelo has painted his own face,
elongated and grotesque in the folds of the pelt.

Self-portrait as shucked flesh,
dragged to the judgment:
Bartholomew glowers, knife aimed at Christ
or at the Virgin, who recoils
from the damned gnawed by demons, or else
from the raised, damning hand of her Son—

Shall we haul
the flayed skin into paradise
(angels flying the thorn
crown and sponge and pillar of flagellation)

*as long as people continue to see me*
*after I'm dead*

the wrinkled face in the pelt,
the serpent's tongue tattooed behind the ear?

*Flesh and blood cannot inherit the kingdom,*
*nor does the perishable*
*inherit the imperishable . . .*

# J

Lo, I tell you a mystery:

three thousand embryos, frozen in nitrogen,
unclaimed for five years at in-vitro clinics,

are slated for destruction today
with a drop of alcohol on each.

*We live in samsara*

*and spacing out about nirvana*
*doesn't help anyone,* says

a teenaged Tibetan lama
who's joined a Wyoming street gang
(*if some butthead pulls a gun on His Holiness,*
*you can bet some bodyguard's*
*gonna pop a cap*
*in his ass*)

who, between homework and Little League and chores
sneaks in his spiritual counseling,
*sucking out the bad air*
*and breathing in the pure*

*like an air conditioning repair dude . . .*

Pure air, frozen
nitrogen, three thousand
embryos each the size of a grain of sand.

*A wholly desacralized cosmos,*
I read in Eliade,
*is a recent discovery*
*in the history of the human spirit.*

## K

By the boathouse's
crumbled pylons,
starfish wallow in low runnels of surf—

when I jab them
with a stick, they clutch it

to their nubbed bodies, trying to take it in . . .

So the numinous
closes around whatever
phenomena happen to stab it

and clutches,
piece by piece of its star.

## L

*A universe seething with life*
*billions of years ago—*

NASA on the radio, carbonate
globules in a meteor

from Mars, Earth itself
seeded by supernal life, perhaps.

We hear it as we drive to the Ballard Locks
where the sockeyes

hurl their battered bodies up the fish ladder,
its twenty-three steps, artificial falls

that repel and attract their surge.
In the Viewing Room, the salmon

beat their way uptide, through a tank of churned bubbles
like Serrano's four-gallon tub of urine

haunted by its plastic crucifix:
god who can't leave matter alone, descending

into what craves
transcendence—

and our urge
upward to return to the place

of our spawning—
*universe seething with life*—the sockeyes,

skin ripped, muscles taut with leaping, fight
to spew eggs and milt in a gravel run, where hunks

of flesh will drop off
in the stream where the smolts came from,

once the starved, gill-heaving spawners have driven,
having smelled their way back to its rock.

# O

*Why does this generation*
*seek a sign:*
Cross–shaped

blister of sunlight
photographed over a cove
just before three Catholic children

drowned there in riptide: its white
trail of bisecting lights
hung, grained-out and glowing, over the beach.

At the soup kitchen, the volunteers
crowd around a blown-up
print of it, souvenir from the funeral:

*I just don't agree it's the Angel*
*of Death waiting*
*to get them,*

one volunteer grimly shakes her head,
*I don't think it's Death,*
*it's Jesus . . .*

# S

*I implore that my Work may be sprinkled*
*with the Blood of the Lord Jesus Christ:*

So Cotton Mather begged God
*with daily Cries*
that the publishers should want his Church History.

—Reading, alongside Mather, my own galleys,
fretting about what the blurbs would say,
what the editors would say,
what the reviews would say,
every night another dream
of the book's
release: *Piss Christ* on the cover, or my mother's quilt
(in the dream I write it as *guilt*)

or inksmears where the blurbs should be—

   T

Book of Merits, Book of Faults,
blackened by centuries of candlesmoke:
in the Last Judgment, the fresco's

angels eternally unroll the scrolls,
and the Blessed
quiver to hear their names.

Versions of the holy—
*my agent
has three manuscripts of mine, she really thinks I'm hot,*

*you know
it's a prestigious award I've just won . . .*

My back
jacket, filled in with its praise

*sprinkled with the Blood
of the Lord Jesus Christ*

—Starfish
wallow in their crack of rock, wrap
their five arms

around whatever seems to them like food.

## U

Envy: two slugs on a mound
of fresh dogshit,
chewing their way back to the ground.

## W

*For admiring myself,*

*I loathe myself,*
Michael Wigglesworth wrote in his diary.
The unspeakable

conversation of judgment:
In the Sistine Chapel, St. Peter
cocks the round barrel of his enormous
key to the kingdom
and aims it straight at Christ

*(I don't think it's Death it's Jesus)*
who floats
in His yellow bubble,
hand raised in a gesture
of benediction, or damnation, I'm never

sure which. *Munday I found pride
monstrously prevailing;*

*Tuesday so much secret*
*joying in myself, plague-sores*
*running day and night . ..*

—All August,
staring at Michelangelo's judging
angels, eyes rolled up in their heads,
I loathe

myself for my self-loathing.
These accounts I can't keep
keeping: sins
deducted from graces, rejections
from publications
*So that people continue to see me*
*after I'm dead—*

Book of Faults
with a fissure down its middle, as though
the wall itself couldn't bear
the weight of its blame.

## X

In my Father's house, so many closed-up rooms.
Such slitted attic windows where I find

myself, gazing downward at the garden,
its stunted boles and chewed leaves,

sunflash on the washed and dented Mazda.
In dust-shaft light, dim

buzzings deep in the rafters, over rusted
nails, a cracked jar. Kingdom and fine city.

Lord, rouse yourself for me now, in this sealed
heat, mildewed air, where the soul

hoards its gatherings through the smudged
dust of half a summer, forgotten

souvenirs, windows
gold with another year's pollen.

Sizzle of shorted
wires, spark-flash

like firefly in the far loft: even
here, Lord, in the stagnant attic,

you're nested, driven, swarming
under damp shingles

to a chambered and nectared hive.

## Z

How secret
the overlay
of the sacred—tracks
of the Holy Ghost

by the dredged
harbor, the gnarled
and peeled madronas.
Everywhere I look, even

in Andres Serrano's
photographs of the morgue: the lush
scarlets and clumped blacks
of the burn victims' skins,

their hands
blotched with fingerprint ink,
the pictures laid end to end, fingers
almost touching, like God

and Adam in Michelangelo's Creation,
the divine spark reimagined
as flesh-charring. So
*kenosis:* God's

emptying himself of divinity
to take on this marrable
body. Piece
by blasted piece,

the profaned
days are hauled up again,
barnacled and briny,
glinting as they sink

back. Twenty-first
Sunday in Ordinary Time:
I bless myself, and move on,
holy water dripping from my fingers.

*—Summer 1996*

# from *The Monstrum Fugue*

fugue: <Latin *fugere,* to chase, *fugare,* to flee:
*1. a polyphonic composition, constructed on one or more themes*
*introduced from time to time with various contrapuntal devices*
*2. a flight from one's own identity . . . a dissociative reaction*
*to emotional stress, during which all awareness of personal*
*identity is lost*

*There are several things that cause monsters.*
*The first is the glory of God.*
—Ambroise Paré


## HOST

Imperfect
split of the ovum, flesh
fused, half doubled, half severed
*So the trumpettour soundit at such tyme*
*as the people sould cum and sie the Monster:*

Lazarus Colloredo,
the Italian Gentleman Pregnant
with His Brother

*that grows out of his navell*
*He carryes him at his syde*

Shrivelled
John Baptista, *which was borne with him,*
*and liveth still,* with rudimentary
genitalia, shared
viscera, liver, milt, &c., three fingers
on each hand, head
drooping backwards, torso half-
emerging, one leg
still buried in Lazarus's side

118

*It had a kynd of lyf, and feilling*

Sagged
lids. Feather-
stir to show he breathes.

Unsplit
into the imperfect, division

being wanted—

cognate: Lat. *com* (together) + *gnatus*, born
imperfect split

And the other

joined rupture:
multiple personality's
polyfragmentation, the psyche's
self-twinning, and twinning, in trauma, its
scattering the horror among the sharded
amnesiac selves,
each the keeper of one memory *(a kynd
of lyf, and feilling,
it liveth still)*

A deadbolted
room has been found
in Violet's mind, stinking
always of Lysol: the alters
huddle outside the door.
She's still
twelve in there,

gone mute from screaming unanswered for twenty years.

The multiples
watch from inside,
even when no one knows
they're there,
even when they can't speak . . .

Cum and sie the Monster,
multiplied,
both joined and separated:
Monster: <Lat. *monstrare,* to show, *monore,* to warn: a grotesquely
    abnormal fetus or infant
Monstrance: <Lat. *monstrum,* portent, monster: a receptacle that
    holds the Host

                              (grotesquely
abnormal, twinning, and twinning:)
Host: the consecrated bread of the Eucharist
Host: an organism that harbors a parasite
Host: a great multitude, as *a host of angels*
Host: in Multiple Personality Disorder, the alter personality
    most frequently in control of the body

Letter
from an alter to its host:
"I am the Stranger Within.
I possess and rule absolutely
all your thoughts and actions.
Your body is merely my mask for survival
amidst this gruesome world of humans . . ."

*And Lazarus concealed the body of his little brother*
*by covering it with his cloak*
*so that a stranger would have no suspicion*

*of the monster underneath*

## 2ND ALTER: TO WONDER

The "Two-Headed Nightingale,"
Millie-Christine, born
slave twins, sold
for $30,000 ("for the two
strange lumps of humanity")
tapdanced to their own duets,
one alto, one basso profundo:
"A marvel to myself am I,
As well as all who passes by.
I love all things that God has done,
Whether I'm created two, or one."

*One*
*in conglutination of externall parts*
from the coccyx
to the sacrum

In sideshows, in dime museums,
before Queen Victoria, the double-
monster

danced

(*Themes*
*stated successively by a number of voices*)

Fugue: amnesiac
flight, and forgetting
repetitions
that chase, and flee

Waiting for the doctor
to cut him free,

Eng felt his blood congealing
in his twin's dead body

as he slowly bled to death

                    Divorce
proceedings:
"Daisy is a lovely girl,
but I guess I'm not the kind of fellow
that should be married to a Siamese twin.
I guess I'm kind of a hermit
when it comes to that"

And in a deformed language
draw a resemblance to the soules
deformity

A marvel to myself am I
marvel: <Lat. *mirari,* to wonder at
mirror: <Lat. *mirari,* to wonder at
mirage: <Lat. *mirari,* to wonder at

Skull and scalp
fused, necks
twisted downward so the twins
could never see each other's face

*Whether two, or one*
The mirror's
mirage

wonder: to have a feeling of awe or admiration
wonder: to be filled with doubt

Doubt's
there, in the mirror of wonder,
what wonder

never wanted to see
Cum, and sie the Monster

## 4TH ALTER: THE MIRROR FUGUE

A monster of duplex
symmetrical development
(Millie's heart mirrored Christine's:
one on the right of her chest,
one on the left)

Rectus          Inversus
In Bach's mirror fugues, a motive
stated in the soprano
recurs in the bass,
dominants replace tonics, tonics
return as dominants,
descending melodies reverse-
echo ascending ones

(a monstrance
of doubled
asymmetric development: trans-
substantiant wafer, echoed
in divine descending flesh)

*The Father is with the Son, and the Son with the Father*
*always and inseparably,*

Augustine says. Trying to unsnare the mystery
of the Trinity in words

(he said, in words)
was like trying to pour the whole ocean
into a hollow he'd scraped in the sand.

⚉

A man must leave his father and mother

and *cleave*
unto his wife:

—the Bride
is a Siamese twin—

Lazarus, come forth

Man   and   wife          must                twin
father-and-mother          is             Siamese
his                  Bride          forthcome

un–
      two

twin
twine

            cleave
            leave

⚉

What can't be
contained
in language (*contain*: to hold
together), the way the Father

contains the Son,
and the Spirit
encompasses both,

*always mutually in one another, neither is ever alone—*

(Motive
restated in the bass:)

*Remember God is a multiple, too,*
said a host,
*Father, Son, and Holy Spirit*

                              (The multiples
stare,

descending . . . )

modulates from dominant to subdominant,
from mediant to sub–
mediant
(a showing, a warning
of halved
symmetrical disintegration)

*twin-twin transfusion syndrome*
*hypervolemia in one*
*omphalapagous twin*
*hypovolemia in the other*
*unbalanced shunting within the mutual circulation*

*Urgent separation of the conjoined*
*twins must be undertaken*

## 5TH ALTER: METAPHOR:
## TO TRANSFER, TO "BEAR CHANGE"

In the Ritual of Integration
("'Me' is 'We' reversed")
the twins must be
unblended, reabsorbed
into the body of the host
(the common gastrointestinal tract
divided beyond the terminal ileum,

dissociative shunting–aside
of painful amnesiac affects
must be ablated through undoing
discontinuities of identity and memory)

*They twain*
*shall be one flesh*
no more, cranium
severed, the double
liver
surgically torn asunder,

and the personalities
one by one
weaken, and die
(their blood congealed
in the twin's
dead body)
as the host
reassembles a cohesive memory—

But no
co-
hesion here: even
these metaphors

won't yield
separation:
multiple
personalities, conjoined
twins

cognates

the metaphors
cleaving

(So the double monster
could dance)

How
keep them apart:
Who is joined with an alter named Garbage?
Who fused
by a "sword-shaped appendix"
to a brother already stiffening with rigor mortis?

*Introduce me            to myself*

6TH ALTER: SUICIDE

       (If the double-metaphor
       won't "yield":

In autoimmune disorders, the cells
confuse themselves
for invading

pathogens, antigen
and antibody
deranged, so the

127

"self-tissues"
cannibalize themselves:
Not-I and I

indistinguishable (Who
am we), hyper–
aggressive, so

the Self, double–
monster,
consumes its prey—

LYRIC

Ineliminable

residuum
John Baptista, huddled

in the cloak
Listless, shut–

lidded
Lips stirring as I speak

The voice of One
in the wilderness

From my navel
he has dragged

Half–
emergent (labored

trace of the thorax)
No license

to shew
When the monstrance

is broken
into, when the Host

is split in two          This
is my body               Do

this,                    in memory
of me                    Lazarus, come

forth                    what
monster                  have you brought

hidden there             what
trumpet                  will they sound

Hallelujah               when the days
are spent                when the Lord

has split                the cursed from the
blest                    at last

in the time of the blending of antonyms:

Nicolas of Cusa: *The place wherein*
*Thou art found unveiled*

*is girt round with the coincidence*
*of contradictories,*

*there Thou mayest be seen*
*and nowhere this side thereof—*

This side, my
side, Baptista's leg

still buried there
Introduce me

to myself
(*intro* + *ducere*: to lead

within) in–
elimin–

able trace          in–
viable terata——

I, Lazarus, gravid
with the swaddled

monster (*always
mutually in*

*one another*), division
being wanted, im–

perfect split, for the
shewing of the glory of God . . .

# MORTOGENESES

*The Corpse Flower: New Poems* (2006)

*forerunner—*

# The Corpse Flower

—Hothouse
stink of inflorescence

as the purple, nine-foot-
tall spathe unfurls to waft

its fetors of fish-rot,
horse-corpse, burnt cabbage, charred

shit—spirals of thousands
of male & female bud-

tips, aquagreen. Spadix
thigh-thick, & the spathe-frill's

devil's-tongue lick—its sheath
exposing the cone: bruise-

maroon interior's
pattern of spattered blood.

∞

Thermogenesis: stalk
fever-soused to the touch

oozes hot oils & puffs
their stenches from its spike

& skirt, its uncurled shroud,
tuber surging by six

inches a day. *Amor-*
*phophallus titanum:*

amorphous, labial–
folded & engorging—

∽

Its half-mile heat-odor
call to dung beetles &

flies & sweat bees' swarm. Duped
scavengers, death-smell-drawn,

refecundate its stalk,
pollen gummed all over

their furred feet. Ascending
already-withering

spathe: summoned, like me, by
the deceiver's rancid

aphrodisiac air,
its swollen & velvet

wet inside . . .

∽

—Carcass

scent in a ravishment
of petal: official

flower, once, of the Bronx . . .
The botanist who found

its simultaneous
rankness & seven-year-

rare bloom, in Sumatra,
was named *Odoardo*

∞

Odor of dead tongues left
to canker in the sun:

*bhel–*: to bloom, to swell. Whose
derivatives *refer*

(bole, bowl, boulder, balloon,
boulevard, phallus, balls)

*to many round objects
& thus to tumescent*

*masculinity*

∞

—& the virgins
collapsed at Kew Gardens

having beheld its slow
erect pulsations, blow

of arousal & rot

∞

—Thanatos-
ic, venereal, its

rut done, it droops into
pollinization, corm

retracting its vulval
quicken & upflush: corpse-

flourish, infloration
of words: *bleed, swell, amorpho-,*

*blow*—raised calyx's three-
day-bloom, propagated

by decoyed swarms of
death-hungerers (flush, flor-

id, flourish, flower, spurt)—
to point us to this mess

of overteeming sur-
vival, luxuriant

deviance . . .

# *Is*

. . . *being is twofold . . . Being conveys the truth of a proposition which
unites together subject and attribute by a copula, notified by this word "is,"
and in this sense being is what answers to the question "Does it exist?"*
—Thomas Aquinas

*When Eve was still in Adam, death did not exist.
When she was separated from him death came into
being. If he enters again and attains his former self,
death will be no more.*
—The Gospel of Philip

Male and female He created them            'is and 'issa
*bone/flesh*              *of my*           *bone/flesh*

—Stripped
in the woods
crouched in the charred                    *Naked came I*
twelve, hard, and scared of it,            lightning-gutted pinetree,

feeling what it felt to touch myself
till the blood rushed, and the shiver
rose, and the change
came on, I could just barely hold back . . .  *Woman, what have I to do
                                               with thee?*

&

*Like a little dick inside,*               she said, not showing me

*Girls have a little spot that's*          *like a dick:*
Like a long splinter (I imagined it)       stabbed inside, blue, half-
                                               visible
under the skin                             gone soft and snaking up
through their bellies,                     a Thing


137

like mine                                    *It's a penis*, my father said,
                                             drunk, his only
                                             version of the Facts of Life,
*don't call it your Thing anymore,*          *it's called a penis . . .*


                                             Vulva: from *volvere*, to turn
                        penetrate: to pierce, to grasp the inner meaning of

Learning the turned–
inward, the con-
volute                                       Tampon-string

the undivulged

I /upreared                                  S /encoiled
                                             lips inside lips

                                             Differ: to dis-ferry, to carry

apart

            ✃

And the copula (the *link*) carries together—dissolves difference—x *IS* y
              One in Being
as in metaphor, that rut of words, that
lust across the copula . . .

As out of the burning,
unconsumed bush
to Moses It said:

I am who am
Thus shalt thou say, I AM hath sent me unto you

—pure Being, or pure
metaphor, or
tautology (say the same say the same)     *Is* is *is*
Then pure                                  profusion
(fruitful: multiply)                       in whatever form It *Is*—

So, in the storm cellar, yeast-smell of my breadmold lab, fuzzed
piecework of black and GI Joe–green,
stale bread crusts in rows
of wooden bowls                            How strangely the patterns
*differed*, side by side:                  pinkish peach-fur on one,
black whiskers, pubic thatch on            the next

Mold–spores called out of the air, the rank
fecundity made visible, in three days—

I couldn't stop                            laying out the molds on my
                                             slides,
under microscope,                          threads and runners and
                                             webs,

couldn't stop breeding                     my apricot and golden
                                             hamsters,
at eleven, waiting                         night after night for *estrus*,
the sniff, the telltale lifting of the tail     (Latin *oestrus*: frenzy)

In the medicine cabinet, my mother's
little silver, punched–out packet of pills    *She takes them so she can fuck*
                                                *with Daddy*

The female's hissing,    her bared incisors,    a grinding of the teeth

It is                          so that it might be                    *Is*

My grandfather's *Playboys*, in their stash, by his whiskey cabinet,
    behind his pirate's sword with the blood-spot, in the long
crawlspace:
my parents caught
me looking, and made me stay down there and look

so I'd know they were upstairs knowing
I was turning the glossed pages
(*and I was ashamed                    and hid myself*)
string of pearls around the nipples and the flicking tongue . . .

"After mounting, the male                    becomes tired and
disinterested"

The hamsters frenzied again on their separate wheels

            ∞

In "our" image, male and female            Split, and teeming
                                            out of that one "Am"
*So she can fuck with Daddy you know that's what they're doing when they say*
*they're "taking a nap"*

*Inwardly penetrated and inflamed*
*by divine love,* says Richard of St. Victor, *the soul*
*passes utterly into that other glory*—

That *Is*, penetrant and burning

God's unspeakable name
made out of the *imperfect*
of *to be,*

vowel-less merge:
Y H W H
I am whoever I will come to be

`ıs/male                                          `ıssa/fe-male
                    *is*, the fastener

To *grasp*                                    the inner meaning
                    of that "other glory":
*We have our own little spot*
                              *That's why it feels good to us too*

          ∞

Under the dripping water-spout, behind the bars,
    the day-old litter
bled: torn-
off foot in the mother's mouth, and the naked,
pink, uneyed babies
squirming, still, toward her teats—

The runt
stuffed kicking in the mother's cheek-pouch as she
gnawed—

*It's just how Nature*
*works*, my mother kept saying,
whiskey on her breath, lifting
the mangled bodies out with a napkin,
*It's just how Nature works*,
her face
contorted above me.

          ∞

When Eve was still                    in Adam,
when death had not                    "come into being"
breasts and vulva buried there inside his sealed-in rib

     —Calling
out of the body of the bread (sopped
crusts, in their trapped-air Mason jars) the invisible
teeming,

and out of the Fungus Book, the language I loved:

rhizopus
nigricans,

mycelia, sporangia, hyphae—

*Spora*, seed           *Sporas*, scattered

—The much-warned-
against           "noctural emission": being
told

by *Moving Into Manhood*      our bodies

were seeded now,        and seeding

White-eyelash threads      over thistledown mats of
spread black
Split spore-cases, on the wet   Wonder Bread

All the girls         single-file
leaving the auditorium     pushing open its red velvet
drapes
their hushed, barking laughs,  the nurse
leading          What were they told

    *Don't call it a "Thing"*
E-
missions

—Pearls
on the nipples, pearls on the tongue . . .

&

Nature's-works: the littering, the
waste, flashlight
on my new, barely visible, pubic hair, in Boy Scout camp,
    in the tent:

*Don't be shy, guy,*
the sixteen-year-old said,
*I may have more of what you've got*
*and you may have less of what I have*
*but we've all got the same*
*stuff . . .*
(A little spot,
a little dick inside . . .)

Who I am, I Am,

copula: reach
hither thy finger.

&

How deep does the *is*                          in the sentence
penetrate,                                      with what *quick*ness
does it burn,
              the copula, the subject and predicate's
                          fuse?
as the mold and bread are made one:     root-cases digging
                                         through the grain,
as I imagined for a while my sister,     with her
Thing                                     all coiled inside—

My mother's face
as she turned away, bloodied
napkin in her hand

Then all night the hamster's
wheel-screak, her gnawed
wood-bar, smell of afterbirth
she never even licked off the litter.

—Then metaphor's
quick copulation
(hiss, sniff, lifted
tail), its resistless                    thrusting-into-one—

          (breadmold, bred hamsters, Yahweh
                 breeding out from His *Is*)

Crumble of mold-dust                as the taken bread
disintegrates                            What's left of the host

body?, when the change

comes

I am Am

Sporangia everywhere,                bursting

# Not Light nor Life nor Love nor Nature nor Spirit nor Semblance nor Anything We Can Put into Words

—Meister Eckhart, on God

As the ellipse
of a zero

is to nothing. As
the starfish's

five sucker-tips
are to the mussel's valves

they wrench open, as its
inverted, flung-

out stomach
is to the mussel's meat.

Or as a glacier to the hiss
and crumble of its calving.

As the foghorn
to the offing, no:

as the offing's
visibility, to the fog.

As cadence, to caesura.
Or insomnia

to obsessive dream.
As et cetera

to what's unmentioned,
incognito

to the name. As the *difference*
to the subtracted–

from. As loess
to sirocco,

bioluminescence
to the murk.

As arthritic
fingers to the etude, as

bone-grind
to arthritis. As a saint's

gnawed jawbone
to the reliquary's

purple felt. As *alienation*
*of affection*

is to *flesh of my flesh,*
*bone of my bones.*

As breath to pleura. As
as is to *as*, I am to You, as

the clitoral
hood, to the tongue.

# And Go into the Street
# Which Is Called Straight

*And the Lord said unto him, Arise, and go into the street
which is called Straight, and enquire in the house of Judas
for one called Saul, of Tarsus*
—Acts 9:11

*The street called Straight is straighter than a corkscrew,
but not as straight as a rainbow. St. Luke is careful not
to commit himself; he does not say it is the street which
is straight, but "the street which is called Straight."
It is the only facetious remark in the Bible, I believe.*
—Mark Twain, *Innocents Abroad*

(*frangere:* Latin, to break)


Go: fraction, fragile, frangible, infringe—
the relatives of *refrain*, sharers

of *fracture*'s fracturing. To *repeat*
is to *break back*. To repeat is to break

back. And the obsessive refrain
(vanished awhile)

I hear now again, like birdsong: backlit, echolalic.
For years it has broken

back and back
in my mind, in moods like this, to murmur

*Half, Half
in love, in love with easeful*

what. To insist I see again,
in the Roman cemetery, each slashed-

in-marble letter (each shadow in the words' gash)
of Keats's epitaph: *Here lies one*

*whose name was writ in water—*
*Writ in water*

chiseled forever into stone.
Engraved. In fractures. Here, lies: *chisel*

means, too, to swindle, to cheat.
Half, half-in-love, half-in-love with easeful

who. *When I have fears*
*that I might cease.* Glean

my teeming. Ease the burden
of always turning,

unmendable, back again, into words. One's name
in water writ. Or in marble, and the gilded monuments.

Unmended. And denamed. On the serpentine
Street Called Straight, where went blinded Saul.

Where went blinded Saul unto
forgiveness, and the burn of flesh.

And the crooked
shall, amen, be straightened.

Strait the gate, and narrow the way.
Half in love. In water writ. Keats's handkerchief and death-mask.

The handkerchief called handkerchief. The life-mask called
    death-mask.
From his cramped bed he stared at the daisy wainscot

—clots of lung-blood on his pillow—
imagined moldering in the grave, gazing

upward at the daisies—All, all
in love, all in love with easeful

Death. Call it Straight,
that moment of blinding, hobbling

hand-in-hand down the crooked
Street Called Straight.

The refrain's a brokenness, though it reaches back, like Orpheus,
to reattach, saying

Come back, come back, the crooked shall be made straight,
saying Straight is the gate, and narrow the way,

murmuring Rich to die, murmuring
To cease upon the midnight with no,

repeating horse's hooves. The aquiline road.
Where went blinded Saul, bearing

the name of a tormented king, the burden
of his burden, its stuck

song. Fragile
refrain. Straight is not

the way:
to convert is to turn

around. And around again. And around. In the whirl–
current, the barnacle-sharp

inlet where I scrabbled my name
today, with a split

stick in spindrift
froth and spume, in cursive

strands of seawrack, and watched
its letters eddy out of their cove, unravel

around each other and snarl
into the gush, broken

back, broken
up (Half-in-love) *Straitway*

*then Paul preached,*
in the chiseled

water, in the
tide–rips through the so-called Straits.

# The Craps Hymnal

The Cumaen Sibyl welcomed pilgrims and supplicants
in her cave. She'd answer any question, prophesy all
night long. She'd write the answers out on palm leaves,
one word per leaf, and arrange them perfectly on the
cave's floor. And when the supplicant reentered, pushing
aside the cave mouth's door, to read that fate, a gust
of wind from behind would blow the prophesy's leaves
into disarranged, unreadable heaps. Here the word
*swordtip*, here the leaf *beware*, here *die*, their syntax all
severed, their endings multiple and contradictory.

Einstein spent his life denying quantum physics'
bizarrely chance-driven vision of the way the cosmos
is put together. God, he said again and again, does not
play dice with the universe. *God not only plays dice with
the universe*, replied Stephen Hawking decades (and
thousands of experimental confirmations of quantum
theory) after Einstein's death; *He also throws the dice where
they can't be seen.*

My four-year-old son Jin and I were cleaning out an
old apothecary jar where we keep junk—poker chips,
snapped rubber bands, Italian lire, double-exposed
photographs from a booth with a previous client's face
superimposed over mine—and he pointed toward a
buried pair of garish red casino dice, said, *Look, Daddy,
there's paradise—*

The turned cube of each definition, recombinant—

*For years,* wrote Emily Dickinson, *my Lexicon was my only companion—*

*Chance* means *to fall.* So cast the lots where they can be seen.

I cast dice every morning to chance my way into a torn red dictionary with its cover hanging off. A 5, a 5, and a 6 would take me to the oracle of page 556: gyrus; gynoecium; the female reproductive organs of a flower; the magnetic properties of a spinning, electrically charged particle. Elevated convolutions on the surface of the brain.

Therefore, the convolutions of the word. Pair-o'-dice. Their charged spin.

7

## PREFACE

*But the final lexicon,* my lexicon says,
*exists only in the mind of God—*

Then open the bound
red leather of this
provisional & battered
dictionary & enter its chambers with praise,
dice-choice Jubilate:

its temporal
labels, syllabification dots,
secondary variables & subsense
numbers. Its virgules/*small rods*
my rod & shaft
(rod wherewith thou smitest/rod that comforts me)

   —Lexical
journeywork: morphology,
shape of the word. Made
flesh, & dwelt among us.

   The turned
cube of each definition, recombinant
dice: verb, reverberant. Re-
verse: turn back. *But the final lexicon,*
*my lexicon says,*
*exists only in the mind of God.* So be this a pilgrim's
daybook, passages
unbooked, arrival times
unschedulable, destination determined
only at the port of disembarking.


   WITH NOAH WEBSTER WE MUST ALSO ACKNOWLEDGE
THAT THIS DICTIONARY MUST BE LEFT, TO SOME
DEGREE, IMPERFECT.

*PREFACE*: *ROM. CATH. CH.*: A THANKSGIVING PRAYER ENDING WITH
THE SANCTUS AND INTRODUCING THE CANON OF THE MASS

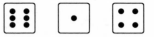

7          9

## *ADMISSION*

Already this forced admission, this
ambiguous witness
borne behind sterilized glass
in the isolette, under jaundice–lights,
after bilirubin spikes,
IV in the neonate's
skull–veins, her
days of refused suckle.

Her whimpering at the bulb's light, un–
fused too soon from the womb's
wall: the ruptured
& shed placenta.

Still fetal, driven from her sac.

Admit
how much you can
spare, if you want
to, Adonai, Lord:
spare, this time, the unripening
fig tree: let fall
limp your blighting grip.


AMNION: A PLATE TO HOLD THE SACRIFICIAL VICTIM'S BLOOD

AND WHEN HE SAW A FIG TREE IN THE WAY, HE CAME TO IT, AND FOUND NOTHING THEREON, AND SAID UNTO IT, LET NO FRUIT GROW ON THEE HENCEFORWARD FOR EVER, AND PRESENTLY THE FIG TREE WITHERED AWAY.

A CONFESSION OF WRONGDOING

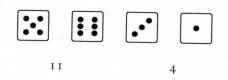

11                                          4

## *ANTIPHON*

Antiphon: canticle's
requisite echo, the divine
Offices reopened. Breviary's

pages loose-leafed,
misnumbered,
vespers at dawn. Antiphonal

call: child's
fever-cry, at midnight, his sopped
quilt. Say again,

Jin, the briefest
of prayers: the hard

glottal stop.

LITURGICAL TEXT CHANTED BEFORE A PSALM OR CANTICLE

SCRUTATOR ALME CORDIUM
(EACH HEART IS MANIFEST TO THEE)
INFIRMA TU SCIS VIRIUM
(THOU KNOWEST OUR INFIRMITY)

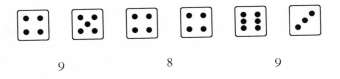

9       8       9

## *REGARDING*

The emergent circumstances require your care—
insist, hour after hour, on your pained

& compulsory regard, regardless
of how little so much that happens has to do

with you, regardless of the self-absolving means
you keep using to justify the end

you never seem to reach, the withdrawing
close of the matter, as though an echo

kept itself repeating in a cave,
walls continually shuddering with its chill

utterance. So Narcissus cupped one ear,
without the least intention of lifting his face

from his face, so illusive there in mud–water,
so self–attracted & attracting

Echo's praises & supplications seemed to him
a hymn to himself, a kind of swelling

background music scored to his every mood
till her body diminished to a voice, repetitious

& vacant of self-regard
as only the unhearable can be.


TO LOOK ON; GAZE; TO HOLD IN HIGH ESTEEM

NARCISSUS' TEARS FELL INTO THE WATER AND DISTURBED HIS
IMAGE. HE CALLED AGAIN, WHY DO YOU SHUN ME?

AND ECHO'S VOICE CALLED, IN ECHO, WHY DO YOU SHUN ME

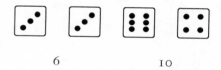

6                          10


## ILLUSTRATION

Ill-used, the Illustrious Ones
dim. All the unmentioned ills

they hoard in mind. They mind, & mind,
the Illustrious Ones

being nothing but minds.
So ignis fatuus, foolish fire,

smolders in their swampland.
Corpse candles, death omens in the bog.

It's said the marsh gas sometimes bursts
into a spectral phosphorescence,

flickering over the mosses
& the never-wet, the swamp's

whole body seething in summer-rot
till all that jungling self–

decay must eventually
combust . . .

*—for Rosina*


IGNIS FATUUS (LATIN, *FOOLISH FIRE*): A PHOSPHORESCENT LIGHT
THAT HOVERS OVER SWAMPY GROUND AT NIGHT, POSSIBLY
CAUSED BY SPONTANEOUS COMBUSTION OF GASES EMITTED BY
ROTTING ORGANIC MATTER

LEGEND THAT IGNIS FATUUS COMES FROM CANDLES HELD BY
CORPSES RISEN FROM THE GRAVE

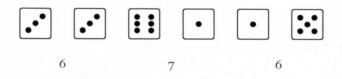

6       7       6

## *LANG SYNE*

The accent of childhood, its

language: lang syne, long gone by.
Landscape of half-stalks, swamped
crops, from the locomotive's

window-flash. In frost
the swathed peach orchards.
Southward, and past-ward, past

what lost Macon drawl
hangs, barn-lantern, filaments
un-candescent. Take me back

there, where the boiling
peanuts thump their tin pot,
where sugar cane's slashed

open in the sun. Necklace
of a thousand snake's rattles
stitched together, the gone

goes, & as it goes, goes on . . .


A PLACE OF NURTURE
TIME LONG PAST

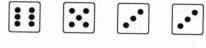

I I                          6


## APOCRYPHA

In the sessions something hidden was made
manifest. & in their Minutes something manifest

secreted—
*Apocryphal:* hidden away.

& so as dreams will work
their manic substitutions, recondite,
I keep working mine: alchemical, the purged
stone. (Scrubbed mud & excrement
off the fractured crystal—)

The quotidian's fool's gold.

In the Apocryphal
Gospel of this February
some gravitational force can only be traced

through what's left warped
by having been so pulled:
ellipsis straining outward toward the strange
unseeable attractor . . .

& some fluent aphasia
maintains its syntax, stutters
through its substituted words:

read *obfuscate* for *clarify*,
*abominate* for *enshrine*.
For *I dread to see you going* read
*How unaccountably*
*soothed I keep feeling now you're gone* . . .


*APHATOS*, SPEECHLESS

IN WERNICKE'S APHASIA, SPEECH SOUNDS EMPTY AND IS LACKING
IN CONTENT AND MEANING. SUBSTITUTIONS OF ONE WORD FOR
ANOTHER ARE COMMON.

"I CAN'T TELL YOU WHAT THAT IS, BUT I KNOW WHAT IT IS, BUT I DON'T KNOW WHERE IT IS. BUT I DON'T KNOW WHAT IT'S UNDER. I KNOW IT'S YOU COULDN'T SAY IT'S I COULDN'T SAY WHAT IT IS."

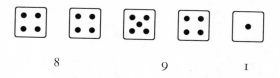

8          9          I

## PILGRIMAGE

All our pilgrimages, peregrinations, & here
we are, listless, folding away our tents.
Even if we should take a permanent

liking to this desert kingdom, chances
are it remains always remote, its subjects
muttering at us in unlearnable tongues.

Now watch the smothering shrine
we fled so far to escape
become, however unwittingly,

the template for a new Temple
where we settle in, eager to adore
again: the same

cherubim in beaten gold, incorruptible
acacia doors, inner
sanctuary's unpartable veil: Holy

of Holies, sacrosanct
exactly because
uninhabitable, unhomely.


A LONG, WEARY JOURNEY, AS TO A SHRINE

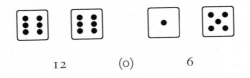

12          (0)         6


## *THROES*

So you dream I cross
red ink through your line
*throes of passion*

—The catechism
forbids us to believe
in our dreams: wicked, since
ungovernable by reason or faith . . .

Not *throes of passion*, those
Harlequin words, but *passion-throws:*
after all, you bring me
in Lent a silver jigger, tintinabular,
two dice rattling deep, exposed in its side

& at Christmas a rosary
you sewed with strings of dice instead
of crucifix & beads—

Artifacts of the ungovernable, the risked
unreasonable throes

162

Sevens, & craps, the hard
odds we take, & faithful, take again . . .


CONVULSION, PAROXYSM, SPASM, AS IN CHILDBIRTH

TAKE: TO PLACE A BET; TO SUBJECT ONESELF TO; TO ENDURE;
TO UNDERSTAND OR INTERPRET

ODDS ARE THE POSSIBLE CHANCES OF THROWING A SHOOTER'S
POINT BEFORE HE OR SHE THROWS A SEVEN

| SHOOTER'S POINT | ODDS |
|:---:|:---:|
| 4 | 2 TO 1 |
| 5 | 3 TO 2 |
| 6 | 6 TO 5 |
| 8 | 6 TO 5 |
| 9 | 3 TO 2 |
| 10 | 2 TO 1 |

TO HURL WITH GREAT FORCE, AS IN ANGER


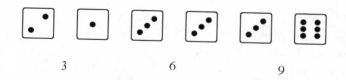

3         6         9


## DEUCE

Deuce, snake eyes, craps, doom-
two—

Deuce-dice, singular & twinned. The two-
fold, deuce, Deus,
craps: sweep the stacked chips away. Deterred
reference, what it *means*.

Snake eyes, the crapped-out, the chants, the
chance, the accident
of two (me, you), the

dual, doomed to
the duel.


A THROW OF TWO IN DICE GAMES: BAD LUCK; THE DEVIL

HAVING A DOUBLE NATURE, CHARACTER, OR PURPOSE

SNAKE EYES:

14                              9

*BALM*

Still you bring
the spikenard, the myrrh
though I swore the odor of such
soothants repelled me

Through the cut bark, your
issue: slather of Gilead-balm, un-
believed in, self-forbidden
resin, viscous, under a clot
of cordiform leaves.

Touch
the bared & secret

164

lesion, you
who hold that blade to the bole.


*SOOTHE*: TO SHOW WHAT IS TRUE

TO MAKE THE WOUNDED WHOLE
TO HEAL MY SIN–SICK SOUL

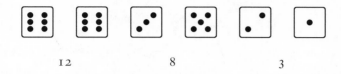

12          8          3


## *VERONICA*

Vera icon, in barbarous
jargon, garble
of Latin & Greek: true
image, Ver–
onica.

Who wiped Christ's brow, who kept
Christ's face:
the fled & hoarded image. Likeness
of the likeness

of the likeness. In the passional, the martyrs' book,
thumb quickly to the last pages, the smudged ones—
there the lance, the whip, the psalter,
fire-barrel, the martyrs
suffering their way in to themselves

so their passion might be forever
memorized, definitional, immemorial.

All these unsustainable likenesses—
Iconoclast, lift your mallet
to the hidden, hoarded statuette.
Of the face in folds of the sopped linen,
Blotter, disbeliever, leave me

no trace.


AND GOD SAID: LET US MAKE MAN IN OUR IMAGE, AFTER OUR
LIKENESS

IN KEEPING WITH LEGEND, THE FACE OF JESUS IMPRESSED ON
A HANDKERCHIEF SAINT VERONICA OFFERED HIM ON THE ROAD
TO CALVARY

"IN THE AMPHITHEATER OF ANTIOCH, THECLA LEAPT INTO A
POOL FULL OF SHARKS WITH THE CRY, 'NOW IS THE TIME FOR
ME TO WASH.' SHE RECEIVED, IN THIS WAY, THE GREAT RITE
OF BAPTISM. A CLOUD OF FIRE SURROUNDED HER, SO THAT SHE
COULD NOT BE SEEN NAKED."

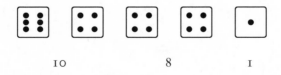

        IO              8              I


## SIC

*Sic:* intrusive erratum, obelus
impugning the spurious
passages in the codices,
interpolations of the lost originals

(interlinear
disputations of authority, so the text
lies & self–accuses, embellishes

& unadorns)

Sick (sic) the hounds
the corrigenda
Let them bay

*Sic passim:* thus
everywhere, unbegotten:
the mistranslated phrases, legendary accretions

illegitimate
theogonies

the corrupted, unattested
uncontainable
variant readings

———————

*corrective
footnotes

diluvium
of the verge

INDICATING THAT A SURPRISING OR PARADOXICAL WORD IS NOT
A MISTAKE AND IS TO BE READ AS IT STANDS

*SIC PASSIM*: THAT AN IDEA IS TO BE FOUND THROUGHOUT THE
TEXT

*SIC* (*V.*): TO URGE TO ATTACK

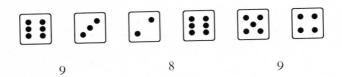

9           8           9

## *REFUGE*

Must it remain so difficult
to recover the referent? Shouldn't the words *refer* us

(carry us back) to some
original source of refuge, some

spoil bank heaped with shucked shells?
Refuse from which came the picked meat,

blue crab, delicacy
difficult of access, yet exquisite.

Must *extravagant* always migrate
back into extra vagari, *wander outside,* or, vagrant, wander

up the page to *extramundane,* outside
the universe or physical world?

Why must the linguistic background
radiation remain unfiltered, so that the total

incident on the surface reflects
& then deflects the extra-

mundane radiant
flux?

REFRAIN OF *REFRAIN*: PAGE 989 A SECOND TIME; WHAT MUST BE
THE ODDS

EXTRAMUNDANE, EXTRANUCLEAR, EXTRAORDINARY,
EXTRAPOLATE, EXTRASENSORY, EXTRATERRESTRIAL,
EXTRATERRITORIAL, EXTRAUTERINE, EXTRAVAGANT

10(0)

## *AMEN*

Cage, in the dead-room, the anechoic
chamber, hearing
only his blood-rush & his nerves.
Unstoppable self-noise. Offering up
intention, as a sacrifice:
*The essential meaning of silence is*
*the giving up of intention.*
*No one* means
*to circulate his blood.*

"Room hermetically sealed
against contingency & echo"

Unidentified
quotations, sounds
disconnected from the occasions of their audition—

Hallelujahs
continual from the amen corner

Amen: half-man, half-ram
His name
means Hidden One

To reproduce silence: Cage's
projected *Silent Prayer* for Muzak, four
minutes of dead air

Hallelujah
Amen
Let us close our mouths & pray

Why do we say, the mystic said,
*I think* but not
*I beat my heart?*


AMEN: EGYPTIAN GOD OF LIFE OR REPRODUCTION

AMEN CORNER: CHURCH SEAT RESERVED FOR PERSONS LEADING
RESPONSIVE AMENS

(HEBREW *ĀMĒN*, CERTAINLY)

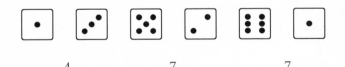

4            7            7

*LAPSE*

Listen,

lapsers, back-
sliders, sublapsarian

goers–after–grace:

the hearable frequencies
stay crowded with sound,
their waveforms' amplitude
archipelagos in the static:

In static, the grace notes,
the untuned waves
of what's–not–listened–for

as unspeakable syllables
spume infrequencies
that articulate the inarticulable,

& the Elect, the Blessed Ones
tune to the interference & listen hard.


DOCTRINE THAT GOD ALLOWED THE FALL FROM GRACE AND
ELECTED SOME OF THE FALLEN TO BE SAVED BY A REDEEMER

I CAN'T TELL WHAT IT MEANS. LISTEN HARD.

IT IS UPON THESE TWO SMALL UNIMPORTANT DICE THAT EMPIRES
ARE BUILT

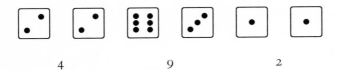

4       9       2

## HORIZON

Shall we end
with the customary reading of the minutes

or with a hard scrutiny of the hours:
infinity sign like a fallen hourglass—

Horologer, sprinkle your sand, measure
precisely its passage through the strictured
chamber severing already

from not-yet. Take
the measure of the measures that we take
to read the minutes, syllable by syllable,
second hand's sweep around the circumference
of the watch.

The watched circumference—

Read the minutiae: *scrutinize*'s
origins in rubbish,
*scrutari:* to rummage in a heap of trash.

Ragpickers, hour-
tellers, watchers: rummage
there, at the celestial horizon, among
the rubbish of the written tongues, at

infinity,
intermingling of the zenith & the nadir.


AT THE INTERSECTION OF THE SENSIBLE AND RATIONAL HORIZONS

IN THEIR MINUTES SOMETHING MANIFEST SECRETED

∞

SANCTUS

# Lord's Prayer

*Cast thy bread upon the waters: for thou shalt find it after many days . . .*
*for thou knowest not what evil shall be upon the earth.*
—Ecclesiastes *11:1-2*


Old One, who art in heaven, the ground's
hacked with rain-dents in ice here,
on earth, choked as it is

through months of mud & dim, threshheld.

Old One, supraliminal,
unfathered &
extramundane:

down how many deep-settled & alien

layers will your hallowing
seep? Daily your bread's cast on the waters
& daily the sops drift in,

algae-scummed, demanna-ing. So the kingdom,

as it comes, disintegrates, grain by grain. Old One,
Tetragrammaton,
unutterable

as thy hallowed & devoweled name,

pass across us, trespass us, like that
squall of crow in the square
as it jabs its beak in the puddle's

174

overlapping circumferences of disturbed

surface, drop by hailed raindrop, smoothed
loose by wind
so it flashes transparent

to the underlamina's burnt-brick glaze

then deflects again, in a skim, the streetlamp's
midmorning flush. Our Father,
unfathering,

be done, be done

with thy will, with its
unbroken last testament. Giver of days
like these, trinkets & tokens, the quotidian's

temptation, all otherwhere occluded:

in the circadian, sleep's
drag & draw through daylong litanies
of sitcom & beer-guzzle &

bedlamp's spluttered *Amen.* So be it,

Old One, half-
lightstreaked & macrocosmic & half
coiled down inside the quanta, imperceptible

ground, evil-deliverable & self-clustering.

As it is
in heaven, let it seem, at least,
as if it were on earth

(the half-flayed sycamore rattling

loose its last seedballs & stalks, as the crow
flaps from the grass-sludge's
hierogram of bootmark & bird-scratch)

visible & inscrutable scrawl,

thine, let it be thine Old One, thy signatory
X: let these dimmed-
out days seem that

much *willed*, unharrowed though it is here, kingdom becoming
& unbecome, amen.

# Rotbox

—*for Thor Hansen*

*Mr. Shiftlet felt that the rottenness of the world was about to engulf him . . .*
*"Oh Lord!" he prayed. "Break forth and wash the slime from this earth!"*
—Flannery O'Connor

## (THE COMPOSING)

Thor tilts the horse's head to pour
off the corruption. Fall
harvest of the rotbox, its mesh

of cage-wire & cement & thigh-
deep wildgrass in a muck
with llama bones & beaver-jaws

& loose-shaken incisors from
some gone creature. Dentist's
picks to scrape all the cartilage

down. Steam off the grass-frost. Sunday
morning complacencies
of groundfog around bleach buckets,

gristle & maggots in hose-blasts.
Rubber gloves, thick. *Women,*
Thor murmurs: *they nag you about*

*bringing home your roadkill, & then*
*they want all the bones.* House
full of whited & reamassed

emu & porpoise skeletons,
headless chimp's recessive
long colonnade of a ribcage.

& the rotbox cage is empty
now, rinsed like the horse head's
scrubbed-out sockets: concavities,

offscum mostly bleached from their eyes.

### (THE DECOMPOSING)

The uncontainable
seepage of the corrupt:

along the grassblades' hoarfrost,
a spatter of marrow,

& driving home from the harvest, my fingers
still chilled & bone-chip-crusted on the wheel.

Stripped off stink-gloves. Jin, four,
thrilled-to-have-news, rushes the door:

*Daddy, the UPS has just
invaded Aff ee gan ee sand—*

& the house is gritted with radio
& TV, war-thrill

over static & the Towers
in replay disintegration, & the bombers

glisten, *whited
& reamassed.*

### (THE REPOSING)

On condition of anonymity
they speak. Of night-vision goggles

& orbiting eyes. Of stealth–jets & destroyers
& Predator drones. Gunships called Spectre
& Spooky. Fifteen-thousand-pound Daisy
Cutters & erupting caves
      *scrubbed-out eyes*

Blastwaves of thermobaric bombs
& slurry explosives in cavemouths
"It's goodbye to whoever is hiding
inside that cave"      *some gone creature*
incinerated or buried alive

"to anyone whose teeth vibrated loose
in the blast
*loose-shaken incisors*
it sends a very powerful message"

& television's rotbox, gone back to replays
& infomercials & *Sunday morning*
*complacencies* (*holy hush* of Eagles & Braves)

*scum* in the *groundfog*, the offloaded

payloads      *recessive colonnades*
of the stripped-down & inhuman drones

    *fall harvest*
*brought-home roadkill*
*poured-off corruption*
*want all the bones*
*offscum*
*bleached*
*away*

# Mortogenesis

*Q: Name the Instruments of Our Lord's Passion?*

The Catechism's parchment—moth-bit shrine:
Its illustrations' crack of lance & rose-
Thorn-crown all staple-ripped along the spine
Like Passion's instruments themselves. Shed clothes,
The red & unseamed silk the soldiers line
Up around the cross, the winning die—who knows
What instruments the Passion strums. Are those
All nails, or plucks for lyres? A sponge of wine
& vinegar uplifted as a sign
Centurions' swords were instruments of shine
& slake & stab, uncoiling hose
Of flagellants' whips: who chose
*Those* instruments of passion? The closed

Catechism's split & mold-splotched gilt . . .

&

Forget that Answer Book. The sky's His skull.

His spit's our rain, englobing mist. P'an-Ku,
Whose spoiling corpse bred forth the universe,

Cosmogeny of rot & humus-bloom,
That world-begetting crumble, regenerate flesh—

—*We're worm-meat*, I keep saying in a dream,
*Dirt-food*, gelatinous brains & craniums

All oxygen & carbon supernova-
Outblasted, star-furnaced & erupted

*—We're star-ash & we're worm-meat all the same—*
From helium cores a billion light years gone:

Nothing the Catechism says on that.
*Here be dragons*, say the contours of the map.

❧

From out of P'an-Ku's vermin humans came:
The fleas & lice that crawled His furred hide.

Primordium of god-spawn—female, male—
Across His bones (the mountains) slunk our tribes.

& now we watch this carcassed multiverse,
Unshrivelled mass & power, gravitons

Deforming space, the vacuum quantum-thick
& mass-creating, mortogenesis

Of cosmos, split eggs of antimass, & only
we vermin-spawn to spell its figures out:

❧

"Quantum electrodynamics reveals
that an electron, positron, & photon

occasionally emerge spontaneously
from a perfect vacuum

permitted by the uncertainty relation
$\Delta E\ \Delta t \sim h$:

Our universe may simply be
a fluctuation of the vacuum . . ."

❦

So bass this music, Passion-plucked, this nail-
On gut-string instrument, discordant,

Staccato. Rip of skin, & tendril-curl,
Louse-creep through fur, His flesh our soil,

Corrupted body breeding. Egg-split. Rood-root.
& now twelve billion vermin eyes look out:

O Skull-for-Sky, what sockets have You got?

# The Vanishing Point

*The painting has vanished. The icon remains.*
—Robert Payne, on Leonardo's *Last Supper*


*To lessen the impact of the blanks,*

a beige watercolor now covers the gaps
where Leonardo's pigment's
unsalvageable,
though for twenty years the restorers have scraped

through centuries of grime
& the refectory's
kitchen-grease,
through the retouched
retouchings, strata of varnish & glue,

as though back down
to the sacral,
the original
turquoise & lapis, the lost
fingerbowls & Judas-
spilled salt—

as though down to the last
supper itself, the first
liturgy of blood & flesh, so mingled
with betrayal
(the decayed restorations
of Judas
flaking away)

what restorer's scalpel can scrape them apart?

        ∞

Napoleon's bored cavalry
scratched out the apostles' eyes,
& steaming dung from their horses
left white streaks of mold down the fresco.
& the monks hacked away Christ's feet
for a more commodious kitchen door,
& an American bomb
crushed the ceiling & apse
all around the sandbagged
Supper, left it
exposed to two years of rains.

& now tourists of the restoration
must walk
through a labyrinth
of glass chambers
with wind-machines & antibacterial carpet
to purify their dust
& bioeffluents
(sweat, dandruff, car exhaust, boot-dirt), to

slow
the inexorable encroachment of the blanks.

&

Christ, at the vanishing point. He's caught
exactly in the cracked
spine of the book where I try to stare down
the chipped image I remember

through scaffolding in Milan. Green
mold over His fingers
as they reach for the bread of His life.
In a half-ripped seam

where the binding's unraveling:
blue robes toward the loaf & the light,
red for Passion toward the wine & the dark, Judas

shoved back from Him as though by a blast.

　　　∞

*If I have been unable to do,*
Leonardo wrote in his notebook, under
"Epitaph": *if I . . .*
& there the sentence
trails away, unfinished
as whatever it was he meant his life to do . . .

　　　∞

"a surface completely ruined,
disintegrating into tiny scales of color
falling off the wall.
It's enough to make a person
want to shoot herself"
　　　　　—the restorer

Vasari, 1556: the Last Supper is already only *a muddle of blots.*

"This is not Leonardo. It is merely
fragments of bottom layers of the underlying original"
　　　　　—critic of the restoration

*Lord, is it I?*

　　　　　　　　　　　　floodwater under the painting
　　　　two feet high

*La pittura é rovinata tutta*

"The question is whether to attempt to recover an original
that is at best in a fragmentary state"

If I have been
unable to do, if I . . .

Drink ye, all of it, for this is my blood

&

Zachary, at the vanishing point. T–
lineage acute lymphoblastic
leukemia. At eight,
Pokémon in his hand,
his face *a muddle of blots*, sourceless
bruises. Feed–
tube through his nose. Ativan
hallucinations. Prednisone
tablets tucked into Jell-o.

Methadone–
wean,
after two months on morphine.
*The chemo's*
*got to get in there & blast*
*all those mean cells away. It's*
*supposed to make you sick, that means*
*you're mowing down all the bad guys inside you*

Verily
the traitor's hand
dips with me, into this dish . . .

&

The underlying
original inside
me, sfumato,
in its smoke-haze of squamous flakes:
if I leach
down to it, with solvents
under microscopes, scalpel-scrub
of disintegrated grime & lacquer, down
to the gesso's
fundament, to
the "grotesquely feminine"
lips of Christ? What's left
if the accretions,
layer by layer, fall away, & the glazed
opacity of the first pigment,
fungus-overgrown, betrayal-mingled, crumbles off the wall?

&

—Dream-stare
into the alabaster masks, no
eye-holes, of the Customs guards,
on the border
of Georgia,
on Zachary's hospital grounds:
& the guard
whose hair is blowing
away, in clumps,
confiding
*It's supposed to feel*
*miserable, like this.*
*That's how you can tell*
*it's made*

*good . . .*

&

Among the possible
modes of failure,

post–remission:
mediastinal mass, recurrence
of blast-cells in the marrow—

Then the requisite
irradiation of the brain
& spinal column where the leukemia's
occulted—

("a more toxic approach
may increase the likelihood of a cure")

Sacrament
demanding blood, & flesh—

        ✀

Re-
touch, Christ, that dipped

sop, that knife-blade in Peter's fist. Pass
over (lamb's
blood on every door)

& over the molting
color-scales. Pass
over Zachary, in his sleep:
bruise by bruise
wipe clean.

*The picture*
*is utterly ruined*

That thou doest, do quickly:

Scour, acid-
burn, down
to the point

of the disease's
vanishing

&

     lying
original
    smoke-haze:
if I leach
         solvent

  disintegrated

fundament
  "grotesquely feminine"
          left

opacity    first
       betrayal

    —Dream-stare

&

When the workmen's
pick-axes loosened whole crusts

of paint, the monks
nailed them back on, so Doubting

Thomas' finger points
now to that hammer-healed

paint-wound
The irrecoverable whole

—A line
of poetry is a chance,

said Hugo Ball,
to get rid of all the filth

that clings to language
—& that crumbles

everything in the cleaning
so that the *point*,

whatever it once
was, vanishes,

like the rice-grains
of Leonardo's lapis, under

microscope, scraped
down & reaffixed

so you can barely tell
what grime's

expunged along the fracture-
lines, what

incrustations
of overlaid varnish & inbred

soot must be suffered
to remain

&

At the point
of origin, also the vanishing:

through www.newprayer.com
a radio transmitter
will set loose your supplication
at the site of the Big Bang
("why not send our prayers directly
to the last known
location of God?")

& hound
down the gone
One

(prepaid account for 20 prayers, $75)

—The diagrammed
perspective lines
toward the vanishing point
at Christ's head: like an assassin's
rifle-sight

Signal-scatter, into the cosmic
background radiation

To transmit
your prayer
to the Big Bang now, click here

&

In the paint's
caesura, the beige
gaps, where any
conclusion whatsoever

may be drawn

what Christ-face
undiscovered underneath
stares & crumbles, waits
still for the traitor's lifted hand?

waits
for the oncologist's lifted hand—

&

Mow down,
Christ, the bad

inside:
amateur-flaws in the overpainting, restoration-
        lies
originations obscured in
        smoke-haze
    if I leech
                    off You,        solve, salve
                    me

    Reintegrate from the
fundament        De
profundis

    &

Should the Supper
(sandbagged, or scaffolded, or trapped
at the glass labyrinth's

core)
be forced to *last*?

Or allowed
its vanishing,
its last-known
location
somewhere among the irradiated

blanks? Set
loose my supplication,
while Zachary's blast cell
count is down
to nothing,

to hammer-healed

Christ,
at the vanishing point, the click,
O-
mega,
the last
Unknowable (restored
to disintegration),

irrecoverable
original,

the last-known . . .


*—for my nephew Zachary*

# ACKNOWLEDGMENTS

From *Spirituals* (Wesleyan University Press, 1988):
"Childhood," "Indian Summer," "At Easter," "The
Reliquary," "Novice," "The Cursing of the Fig Tree,"
"A Dogwood Tree in a Country Graveyard, at Easter."

From *The Creation* (Ohio State University Press, 1994):
"The Creation of Eve," "Eve, Learning to Speak," "Summer,"
"The Instrument and Proper Corps of the Soule," "Eurydice
in Hades," "Arcana Mundi," "Advent: Snow Incantation,"
"Doxology," "After an Adoration," "Sleeping in Santo
Spirito," "Going Home to Georgia," "The Conceiving."

From *Summer Mystagogia* (Center for Literary Publishing,
1996): "Witness," "Sweet Repeaters," "Summer Mystagogia,"
"Primavera," "Ugly Ohio," "Idaho Compline," "The Mono-
logue of the Signified," "A Mythic History of Alcoholism,"
"Ultrasound," "Before Thanksgiving."

From *Signs and Abominations* (Wesleyan University
Press, 2000): "What Did You Come to See," "Negatives
of O'Connor and Serrano," "Hermetic Diary," "Hermetic
Self-Portrait," "Mutating Villanelle," "Errata Mystagogia,"
"Spiritual Alphabet in Midsummer," "The Monstrum Fugue."

And grateful acknowledgment to journals in which the
new poems in this volume first appeared: *Denver Quarterly:*
"[balm]," "[refuge]"; *88: A Journal of Contemporary Poetry:*
"[preface]"; *Field:* "The Corpse Flower," "[lapse],"
"[horizon]"; *Gettysburg Review:* "And Go into the Street
Which Is Called Straight"; *Grand Street:* "Not Light nor Life
nor Love nor Nature nor Spirit nor Semblance nor Anything
We Can Put into Words," "[lang syne]," "[amen]"; *Harvard
Review:* "[sic]"; *Image:* "Lord's Prayer"; *Interim* "[deuce]"; *Iron
Horse Literary Review:* "Pilgrimage," "Admission"; *The Kenyon
Review:* "The Vanishing Point"; *Meridian:* "[throes]"; *Michigan
Quarterly Review:* "[regarding]"; *Quarterly West:* "[antiphon]";
*Shenandoah:* "Mortogenesis"; *Slope:* "[illustration]"; *Southern
Review:* "Is"; *Southwest Review:* "[veronica]."

"Errata Mystagogia" was reprinted in *The Pushcart Prize XXIV: Best of the Small Presses* (2000).

"Is" was reprinted in *The Pushcart Prize XXVIII: Best of the Small Presses (2004)* and in *The Pushcart Book of Poetry: The Best Poems from the First 30 Years of the Pushcart Prize* (2006).

And eternal thanks to my friends who have helped me shape these poems over the years: Zero Hopeloff, Tim Liu, Don Platt, Bill Wenthe, Dan Tobin, Bill Thompson, Brenda Miller, and Robin Hemley.

Bruce Beasley, professor of English at Western Washington University, is the author of five previous volumes of poetry, including most recently *Lord Brain* (winner of the University of Georgia Press Contemporary Poetry Series competition) and *Signs and Abominations*. His poems have appeared in *The Kenyon Review, The Southern Review*, and *The Virginia Quarterly Review*, among other prominent journals, and in *The Pushcart Book of Poetry: The Best Poems from the First 30 Years of the Pushcart Prize*. He won the 1996 Colorado Prize in Poetry (selected by Charles Wright) for *Summer Mystagogia* and the 1994 Ohio State University Press/*Journal* Award for *The Creation*. He has won fellowships from the National Endowment for the Arts and the Artist Trust and three Pushcart prizes in poetry. A native of Macon, Georgia, he now lives with his wife and son in Bellingham, Washington.